THE HEBRIDES
A Mosaic of Islands

Map of the Hebrides

8°W   7°W   6°W   5°W

Sula
Sgeir

North
Rona

— 59°N

Cape
Wrath

Butt of
Lewis

Handa

Flannan
Isles

*Atlantic
Ocean*

L
E
W
I
S

M
I
N
C
H

— 58°N

Summer
Isles

St Kilda

Harris

Shiant
Isles

Little Minch

NORTH
UIST

Monach Isles

S
K
Y
E

BENBECULA

SOUTH
UIST

*SEA OF THE
HEBRIDES*

— 57°N

Canna

Rum

Eigg   MALLAIG

BARRA

Muck

Barra Head

COLL

TIREE

MULL   OBAN

Iona

Firth of Lorne

— 56°N

Colonsay   JURA

ISLAY

Gigha

Mull of
Kintyre

0   20   40   60   80 km

N

THE HEBRIDES
A Mosaic of Islands

J. Morton Boyd
and Ian L. Boyd

Birlinn

This Edition published in 1996 by
Birlinn Limited
14 High Street
Edinburgh EH1 1TE

The Publisher acknowledges subsidy from the Scottish Arts Council
towards the publication of this volume.

THE HEBRIDES
ISBN 1 874744 55 6–A Habitable Land? (Book I)
56 4–A Natural Tapestry (Book II)
57 2–A Mosaic of Islands (Book III)

A CIP record of this book is available
from the British Library

Printed and bound in Scotland by Bell & Bain Limited

FOR LAUREN

What would the world be, once bereft
Of wet and of wildness? Let them be left,
O let them be left, wildness and wet;
Long live the weeds and the wilderness yet.

Gerald Manley Hopkins

Contents

Preface and Acknowledgements

The Hebrides—a mosaic of islands (H-AMI) is substantially Part II 'Studies of Islands and Species' of the HarperCollins New Naturalist volume *The Hebrides—a natural history*. Chapter 1 is new, but the core of the book is Chapters 11–16 of that previous work. This book has two companions: *The Hebrides—a habitable land?* (H-AHL) and *The Hebrides—a natural tapestry* (H-ANT), which are respectively Parts III and I of that previous work. The three books now have independence, but their common origin in the New Naturalist volume, now out of print, gives them an interdependence as a comprehensive review of Hebridean natural history. This specific book deals with the distribution of species among islands while the others deal with the human dimension of the natural history (Volume 1) and the structure of the archipelago (Volume 2).

Morton and Ian Boyd are a father and son team, and it could be said that the work of which this is a part has been forty years in the making. Morton might never have attempted it had he not collaborated with Fraser Darling in the writing of an earlier New Naturalist volume *The Highlands and Islands* in 1964. From the inside, as it were, he could see the great advantages of having the book written by a single author, not just for style of writing, but also for the artistry of compilation of a single comprehensive work from a wide variety of sources. The alternative is to compile a book with many experts contributing one or more chapters, but the result would be very different from the type of books produced by some of the authors of classical natural history books—F. Fraser Darling, E. B. Ford, C. M. Yonge, W. H. Pearsall, Dudley Stamp, Alistair Hardy and others in the New Naturalist series. These authors were at once experts in a limited field, and naturalists of broad erudition and experience. They were able to see and describe nature in the round.

When *The Hebrides* was in its early stages of production Morton's time was taken up with his final years as the Director (Scotland) of the Nature Conservancy

Council and then, in the later stages, by the need to conserve his energies because of an illness. Through this period he needed an assistant to help with the compilation, primary drafting and editing of his text, the incorporation of expert comment and the application of the judgement and taste of a younger scientist. Morton did not require to look further than his second son, Ian Lamont Boyd. Ian made his first visit to the Hebrides in infancy, and came face to face with a grey seal, the animal which was eventually to be the subject of his Cambridge PhD dissertation, for the first time at the age of 19 months. Throughout his boyhood he was continuously on foot with his father in the Hebrides and later, like Morton, had the benefit of a broadly-based Degree in natural science from a Scottish University. Ian has pursued a career in scientific research and is now in charge of seal research at the British Antarctic Survey.

Both hardback and softback editions of *The Hebrides* went out of print within 18 months of publication in 1990. HarperCollins decided not to reprint, but made the book available to Birlinn for reprinting in three shorter books. The authors, therefore, have restructured *The Hebrides* and have provided new Prefaces, Chapters, Bibliographies and Indexes for all three new books. The chapters of the original book have been reprinted with a few amendments; it has not been possible, on account of cost, to update the text of 1990.

The authors were faced with a vast span in geological age, an enormous number of distinct forms of life all of which are specially adapted to their living quarters, a wide range of temperate maritime habitats and a group of human influences and impacts on the environment rooted in Celtic and Norse cultures, and strikingly different today from those in mainland Britain. The whole great assembly is dynamic. It is not sufficient, therefore, to provide a snap-shot of nature and human affairs today: one also has to apply the dimension of history and unrelenting change. To achieve this in three short volumes it was a matter of, firstly, choosing how much to include of the available knowledge; secondly, consulting with specialists with knowledge about the subject of each chapter; and thirdly, incorporating these experts' comments.

The authors are deeply aware that the shape and content of this book and its two companions are a matter of personal choice. It has been difficult to decide what should be excluded; there are many studies which deserve mention and which, in the hands of other compilers, would find a place. The fact that some works are restricted to a mention in the Bibliography does not necessarily reflect their importance in natural and human history. The authors thank the following who have provided valuable unpublished information and other special advice in the writing of this book and its two companion volumes: R. N. Campbell for the distribution lists of brackish-freshwater fishes, amphibians, reptiles and mammals in Appendix 4; A. Currie and Mrs C. Murray for revising their list of vascular plants; the Department of Biological Sciences, University of Stirling for a copy of *Mariculture Report 1988*; Professor P. A. Jewell for data on Soay sheep at St Kilda; Scottish Natural Heritage for a copy of *Agriculture & Environment in the Outer Hebrides* and, together with the Seabird Group, for data from the Seabird Colony Register; Dr M. A. Ogilvie and Dr D. A. Stroud for data on wintering geese; Miss M. G. Roy for helpfully abstracting climatic data from *Scotland's Climate* (Meteorological Office, 1988). Advice on Gaelic literature and names of flora, fauna, rocks and minerals has been given by Ailean M. Boyd.

The authors also thank the authors of papers in the two volumes in the *Proceedings of the Royal Society of Edinburgh* (1979, 1983) which were a rich source of material for these books and A. R. Waterston (1981) without whose efforts the natural history of the Hebrides would remain scattered and inaccessible. We also thank the following for advice and practical help; K. J. Boyd, N. R. Boyd, R. D. Cramond, Miss A. Coupe, Mrs H. G. Foster, Sir Charles A. Fraser, R. Goodier, F. Hamilton, Mrs S. Scott, Prof. A. D. McIntyre, Dr D. S. McLusky, Dr D. H. Mills, Dr H. Prendergast, and others.

Over almost forty years, many naturalists who have not been directly involved in the writing of this book, have shared with Morton their knowledge of the Hebrides. The authors have in mind colleagues in the Nature Conservancy (1957–73) and Nature Conservancy Council (1973–85)—especially J. C. (later The Viscount of) Arbuthnott, M. E. Ball, R. N. Campbell, A. Currie, Dr W. J. Eggeling, Dr D. A. Ratcliffe, J. G. Roger, and P. Wormell; the members of the Soay Sheep research Team at St Kilda (1959–67)—especially Prof. P. A. Jewell and Dr C. Milner; the Grey Seal Research Programme at North Rona and Harris (1959–69)—especially R. Balharry, R. H. Dennis and J. MacGeoch; the Rum National Nature Reserve (1965–85)—especially Dr T. H.

Clutton-Brock and Miss F. E. Guinness; and the Sea Eagle Reintroduction Project (1975–85)—especially R. H. Dennis, J. A. Love and H. Misund. We wish to take this opportunity of thanking them and saluting them for their knowledge of natural science and their contribution to the conservation of nature in the Hebrides.

The typescripts and proofs were corrected by Mrs W. I. Boyd, Mrs S. M. E. Boyd and R. D. Cramond. The authors also wish to thank the following who kindly read and commented on one or more chapters of this book and its two companion volumes—an asterisk denotes more than one chapter. Miss. S. S. Anderson, R. S. Bailey, M. E. Ball★, Prof. R. J. Berry★, Dr J. L. Campbell, R. N. Campbell★. Dr T. H. Clutton-Brock, R. D. Cramond★, A. Currie★, Dr D. J. Ellett, Dr C. H. Emeleus★. Dr P. G. H. Evans, Dr R. J. Harding, Dr M. P. Harris, Dr G. Hudson, Prof. P. A. Jewell, G. S. Johnstone, R. C. B. Johnstone, A. J. Kerr, J. Lindsay, Dr R. A. Lindsay, J. A. Love, Prof. A. D. McIntyre, H. McLean, Dr D. S. McLusky, Dr P. S. Maitland★, Dr J. Mason, Dr A. Mowle, S. Murray, Prof. T. A. Norton, Dr M. A. Ogilvie, Dr R. E. Randall, Prof. W. Ritchie, Miss M. G. Roy, Dr D. A. Stroud★, Dr D. J. Smith, Dr M. L. Tasker★, Miss V. M. Thom, Dr P. J. Tilbrook, A. R. Waterston, Dr C. D. Waterston, Dr R. C. Welch, and P. Wormell★.

J. Morton Boyd
and Ian L. Boyd
Balephuil
Isle of Tiree
Argyll

Islands and Geology

CHAPTER I

These bare stones bring me straight back to reality.
I grasp one of them and I have in my grip
The beginning and end of the world.

Hugh MacDiarmid

An island can be compared to a gemstone set in a silver sea. It is unique—there is none other exactly like it! It is precious—there is a compelling beauty in its scenery, rocks, life and solitude. It is ever changing in the daily and seasonal cycles of nature, but in its hard core it is the enduring Rock of Ages. The Hebrides are a scatter of such gemstones each with its own intrinsic sparkle—each with its own place in Creation, and each contributing an irreplaceable piece to a great tectonic mosaic.

The rocks of the Hebrides are a geological mosaic of great complexity which is seldom exceeded in variety of ages and structures by other archipelagos of comparable size. The celebrated volcanic and coral islands of the Atlantic and Indo-Pacific—Madeiras, Canaries, Tristan da Cunha, Seychelles, Mascarines, Galapagos, Hawaii, Tahiti, and Fiji—have their biological wonders, but none have the range of geological interest possessed by the Hebrides. The Hebrides stands tall, geologically speaking, in having exposed rocks which span all of geological time, and displaying a comprehensive array of geological processes. The age of the Earth is ca 4,600 m.y. (million years) since its primary gaseous existence in the Solar System. The time-span of the Hebrides is almost 3,000 m.y. to the present, and is broadly constructed in four major crustal structures, which follow each other in the geological history of the islands: the Lewisian-Torridonian basement, the Moine—Dalradian metamorphics, the Mesozoic sedimentaries and the Tertiary volcanics.

The Lewisian-Torridonian Basement

When Hugh Miller, stone mason, geologist and evangelist, made his celebrated cruises in the yacht *Betsey* to the Hebrides in 1844–45, he did not have, as we have today, the advantages of a century and a half of geological research to enlighten his appreciation of the islands. Yet, for all that, Miller's mind was possessed by a grandeur of geological heritage as great as any propounded today.

The model of some alpine country raised in plaster on a flat board, and tilted slantways at a low angle onto a basin of water, would exhibit in a minute scale an appearance exactly similar to that presented by the western coast of Scotland and the Hebrides . . . but examination of the geology of the coast, with its promontories and islands communicates a different idea. These islands and promontories prove to be of various ages and origin. The Outer Hebrides may have existed as the inner skeleton of some ancient country contemporary with the mainland, and that bore on its upper soils the productions of perished creations, at a time when by much the larger portion of the Inner Hebrides . . . existed as part of the bottom of a wide sound . . . the Long Island (Outer Hebrides) . . . may have been smiling in the sun when the Alps and the Himalaya Mountains lay buried in the abyss . . . the greater part of Skye and Mull must have been . . . an oozy sea floor . . .

Thus Miller drew a bold interpretation of the rocks of the Hebrides as he and others of his time saw them. Today they are still there as Miller saw them, but the interpretation is different. We now have an understanding of continental drift by the spreading of ocean floors over the past 3,000 million years. The basement of the land which is now Scotland and Northern Ireland was once part of a continent positioned in tropical latitudes south of the equator. Over hundreds of millions of years, this basement moved northward, possibly 500 m.y. ago, colliding with another continental basement, of which England, Wales and southern Ireland were part. Thus the lower strata of the two major geological parts of the British Isles and much of their context (now in Europe and North America, see below) were brought together in tropical latitudes in Devonian times. In the Hebrides, this basement survives in the Lewisian gneiss, ca 2,900 m.y. old, which occupies most of the Outer Hebrides, Tiree, Coll, Iona and Islay, and the water-borne Torridonian sandstones (ca 800 m.y. old) in Skye, Raasay, Scalpay, Soay, Rum, Iona, Colonsay and Islay.

Finely banded, sand-blasted gneiss on the shore at Lossit Bay, Islay, the most southerly outcrop of the Lewisian-Torridonian basement in the Hebrides (Photo: J. M. Boyd)

The Moine-Dalradian Metamorphics

The ancient Lewisian-Torridonian basement was separated from the Moine and Dalradian (Caledonian) massifs of the Highland mainland 525–400 m.y. ago, by a great fault, the Moine Thrust, which runs from the Kyle of Durness on the north coast of Sutherland, through Wester Ross, South-East Skye and southward in the sea bed to the Sound of Iona. Moine schists and quartzites occur in Sleat and in the Ross of Mull and make a minor contribution to Hebridean geology. The Dalradian quartzites, schists, slates and limestones, which are ca 550 m.y. old, on the other hand, make a major contribution to the east of the Great Glen Fault (1,000–600 m.y. ago) in Gigha, Islay, Jura, Scarba, Garvellachs, Lismore and other isles in the Firth of Lorne. Towards the end of the Moine-Dalradian period some 450 m.y. ago, a mass of granite was intruded between the Lewisian rocks of Iona and the Moine schists of the Ross of Mull, towards the southern end of the Moine Thrust. Ross of Mull pink granite makes excellent monumental stone used in the construction of the lighthouse on the Skerryvore and other buildings of distinction in the Inner Hebrides.

The lower Dalradian underlies the rugged, rolling terrain of central Islay, the low undulating island of Lismore and localities near Loch Don, Mull, on the south-east side of the only contact with the Great Glen Fault in the Hebrides. The breakdown of the limestones and the slates in these areas has produced soils of high fertility and good agricultural land. The upper Dalradian is a very different series of rocks which underlies barren, unproductive landscapes. The extremely hard and inert

Jura quartzite partially surrounds the fertile heart of Islay
with a circle of high moorlands, and continues north-
eastwards in the hills of Jura and Scarba, dominated by
the Paps. To the north of Scarba, where the quartzite
becomes thin, the slates occupy much of the Firth of
Lorne, where the slate terrain is seen in a scatter of
islands—Easdale, Luing, Seil, Kerrera, and Belnahua.

The Mesozoic Sedimentaries

Immediately upon these ancient rocks were deposited the
younger sediments eroded from the primeval mountains,
and deposited in sea-filled depressions in the primary
basements. These are the sandstones, mudstones, shales
and limestones of the Mesozoic which hold coal, oil and
natural gas, and many which are fossiliferous. They form
the rocks of the Scottish Central Lowlands and the floors
of the North Sea, Norwegian Sea and seas over the
Hebridean shelf. They belong to the Triassic, Jurassic and
Cretaceous periods, ca 225 to 65 m.y. old, and are found
in west Mull, Eigg, Skye, Raasay, Scalpay, Pabbay,
Shiants and Lewis. These were the rocks sought by Hugh
Miller in his quest for fossils in Eigg, and which he
described as deposited on the floor of a broad sound.
Present within them, there is a prominent succession of
Jurassic strata which consist of mottled clays, limestones,
shales, sandstones and ironstones some 3,000 feet in depth
(now mostly eroded) and ca 180–135 m.y. old. The Great
Estuarine Series of the Middle Jurassic is 600 feet deep in
North Skye, 400 feet in Strathaird, 200 feet in Eigg and
less than 100 feet in Ardnamurchan and Mull. These
strata are the surviving remnants of a petrified coastal
landscape oscillating between marine and freshwater conditions over varying periods of time, possibly originating
from sediments similar to those found today in the coastal
lagoons of Texas and the Everglades of Florida. The
Great Estuarine rocks are widespread. Similar rocks have
been found in north-east Scotland, and others with close
affinities in Yorkshire and southern England.

Hugh Miller reasoned with himself over the alternate
marine and freshwater characteristics of the Middle Jurassic (probably Great Estuarine) rocks at the north point of
Eigg, and found a treasure-trove of fossils.

What has been sea at one period had been lake or estuary at
another. In every case, however, in which these intercalated
deposits are restricted to a single strata of no great thickness, it
is perhaps safer to refer their formation to the agency of

temporary land floods, than to violent changes of (sea) *level . . .*

The hard red beds of Ru-Stoir belong, as I was fortunate enough this evening to ascertain, not to the ages of the Coccosteus and Pterichthys (extinct armoured fishes), *but to far later ages of the Plesiosaurus and the fossil crocodile. I found them associated with more reptilian remains, of a character more unequivocal, than have been exhibited by any other deposit in Scotland . . . in a rolled block of altered shale . . . I succeeded in detecting several shells . . . the small univalve resembling* Trochus, *together with the oblong bivalve, somewhat like* Tellina; *and, spread thickly through the block, lay fragments of coprolitic matter* (fossil dung), *and the scales of teeth of fishes . . . I hammered lustily and laid open in the red shale a vertebral joint, a rib, and a parallelogramical fragment of solid bone . . .*

The Tertiary Volcanics

The landmass destined to become the Hebrides was gradually taking shape. The time was ca 65 m.y. ago. A great depth of Mesozoic strata was resting upon the ancient Lewisian/Torridonian basement. The global position was in low temperature latitudes, and the rift of the North Atlantic, separating the continents of Eurasia and North America, was in progress. The line of rifting lay along the edge of the continental shelf of which the Hebridean shelf is a segment. Between 65 and 57 m.y. ago there was great volcanic activity. The volcanoes of Ardnamurchan, Mull, Rum, Skye and St Kilda, then towering cones, were pouring forth vast floods of lava and fountains of ash and dust, covering the Eocene land-scapes to a depth of over a kilometre in many areas. Thus were formed the third and youngest series of Hebridean rocks on top of the primary Lewisian/Torridonian base-ment and the secondary Mesozoic rocks. They are of three types: the granites and gabbros of the massive volcanic cores; the basalts and rhyolites of the extrusive lavas, cinder and ash; and the dolerites and basalts of the intrusive dykes and sills.

Soaring high above Miller's head as he searched for fossils on the northern shore and lower slopes of Beinn Bhuidhe on Eigg, were the plateau lavas and ash beds, probably associated with the volcanoes in Rum and Skye in the Eocene, ca 60 m.y. ago. These are the rocks which dominate the scenery of the northern Inner Hebrides from the Ross of Mull to the Shiants and at St Kilda. There is also the submarine remains of a Tertiary volcano

Honey-comb weathering of the Jurassic sandstone at Elgol, Skye, showing the overhung, wave-cut cliff, the bedding planes of the sedimentaries, and the Tertiary volcanic rocks of Gars-Bheinn in the background (Photo: J. M. Boyd)

at the Blackstones Bank 50 km WSW of Mull. The Inner Hebrides and Argyll are riven by Tertiary dyke swarms of dolerite and basalt running NW–SE, which cut through all the existing rock formations. These Tertiary rocks are exposed through most of Mull, Skye, Muck, Eigg, Rum, Canna, Sanday, Shiants, St Kilda and, on the mainland, Ardnamurchan and Morven. They produce some of the most famous scenery: the Cuillins, Macleod's Tables, Old Man of Storr, Quiraing and Kilt Rock, all in Skye; Fingal's Cave on Staffa and the Dutchman's Cap in the Treshnish Isles; Ben More in Mull; the Sgurr of Eigg; and Conachair, Boreray, Stac an Armin and Stac Lee, all at St Kilda.

Again we defer to Hugh Miller in his judgement of the Tertiary rocks in their most glorious form: *The Scuir of Eigg is a veritable Giant's Causeway, like that on the coast of Antrim, taken and magnified rather more than twenty times in height, and some five or six times in breadth, and then placed on the ridge of a hill nearly nine hundred feet high. Viewed sideways, it assumes . . . the form of a perpendicular but ruinous rampart, much gapped above, that runs a mile and a quarter along the top of a lofty sloping talus. Viewed endways, it resembles a tall massy tower . . . three hundred feet in breadth by four hundred and seventy feet in height, perched on the apex of a pyramid, like a statue on a pedestal. This strange causeway is columnar from end to end, but the columns, from their great altitude and deficient breadth, seem more rodded shafts in the Gothic style: they rather resemble bundles of rods than well-proportioned pillars . . . The acclivity is barren and stony—a true desert foreground—like those of Thebes and Palmyra; and the huge square shadow of the tower stretched dark and cold athwart it. The sun shone out clearly. One half of the immense bulk before us, with its delicate vertical lining, lay from top to bottom in deep shade, massive and gray; one half presented its many-sided columns to the light, here and there gleaming with tints of extreme brightness, where the pitchstones presented their glassy planes to the sun; its general outline, whether pencilled by the lighter and darker tints, stood sharp and clear; and a stratum of white fleecy clouds floated slowly amid the delicious blue behind it . . .*

The Ice Age and Afterwards

Thus were formed the solid rocks of the Hebrides in their four successive suites. Moved northwards from equatorial to temperate latitudes in their making, the islands, which became a crustal adjunct of the opening of the North Atlantic, were progressively shaped by the elements over the last 11 m.y. The diverse, solid crust has been the medium of a sculptor whose creative genius is seen in the profile and interstices of every island. In Skye, for example, the jagged spires and turrets of the Black Cuillin contrast with the smooth paps of the Red Cuillin, and compose a skyline touching to the human heart and immortalised in song. In close-up, Loch Coruisk is cupped in an ice-carved valley and an inner sanctum to the mountaineer. Closer still, the ochre sandstone surfaces of the Elgol coast, finely weathered to resemble the tracery of a honeycomb, stop the passer-by in wonderment. The actions of ice, sea, rain and river have taken

Raised beaches, West Loch Tarbert, Jura, showing the present shore, and the two levels of raised beach separated a heather-clad scarp and criss-crossed by tracks of large herbivores (red deer, sheep, goats persent) (Photo: J. M. Boyd)

their toll in the erosion of the ancient rocks to screes, gravels, sands and muds. The material has been worked and re-worked by the elements over millions of years, during which time most of the Mesozoic sediments and Tertiary volcanics have been eroded, removed, and deposited in the marine trenches of the Hebridean shelf, and North Sea Basin. The towering volcanic cones of Skye, Rum and Mull, for example, now lie as sediments under the Sea of the Hebrides.

The last ice-age which, at its maximum, covered the whole of the Hebrides (St Kilda probably excepted) with an ice-sheet similar to that of the Antarctic Peninsula today, was the most important of all in the interpretation of the landforms and geology of the islands. It lasted some 15,000 years, and concluded about 10,000 years ago. Its effect was to over-ride the whole land surface with such a depth, weight and crushing movement of ice as to remove all features of previous epochs of erosion, and create a new land surface which emerged from the ice as the Hebrides, approximately as we now know them. 'Approximately', since following the recession of the ice-sheet—which happened in fits and starts, and included temporary advances—the land rose in two main episodes causing changes in sea-level. These changes were in fact the nett effects of a rising of sea-level due to the melting of the ice and the increase in volume of sea water, coupled with the lowering of sea-level due to the uplift of the crust liberated from the superincumbent load of ice. This resulted in changes in the number, size and shape of the islands, and the creation of raised beaches and wave-cut benches. The first rise was ca 25 m and the second ca 8 m. The two raised beaches of even-sized pebbles are widespread on the coasts of the Inner Hebrides. The lower one, for example, carries the esplanades at Oban and Tobermory, and much of the land base of Tiree. Both beaches, the older above the younger, are particularly well displayed in parallel on the west coast of Jura. The uplift of the land also exposed wave-cut rock benches; they can be seen on most of the coasts of the Inner Hebrides, but there are none more conspicuous than that below the 'perched' sea-cliffs upon which stands Duart Castle in Mull, and the neighbouring island of Lismore.

The passing of the ice-age saw a great confluence of ice moving westwards from the Caledonian plateau over and around the Hebrides, gouging as it went the rock basins in which repose the sea lochs, sounds and kyles of the

West Highland seaboard. Whorls of glaciers developed around the mountains of Harris, Skye, Rum, Mull and Jura which were probably nunataks, or rocky islands, protruding above the great Hebridean ice sheet. St Kilda, standing proud of the ice-sheet, also had little strip glaciers. There was a time in the retreat of the ice when the scene in the Sound of Rum probably resembled that of Spitzbergen and South Georgia today. The islands and surrounding seabeds were a depository for enormous drifts of diverse rock carried by the ice from the Highland hinterland, and from island to island. In the south-east of Skye at Allt Annavig, there are major fluvio-glacial deposits expected to yield some 25 million tonnes of sand and gravel. The sands and silts are refined sediments of high quartzite content, while the gravels reflect the geology of the district—gneisses, quartzites, sandstones, granites, gabbros and basalts. This is quite exceptional for the Hebrides, where the glacial and riverine terrestrial deposits are usually sketchy upon a generally denuded, peat-covered landscape. The Ringing Stone, an augite boulder bearing cup marks on the north shore of Tiree, has been rafted there by the ice from some distant igneous origin, possibly Rum. The pebble beaches of the Inner Hebrides consist of glacial material taken from the sea bed by the buoyancy of seaweed growth, tidal and wave action, and cast upon the shores. They are a most glorious miscellany of stones of different origins, ages, minerals, colours, shapes and textures. At a glance, the great geological heritage of the Hebrides is confirmed! Sea-wetted stones on the shore often have a striking beauty, and none more than the 'greenstones' of Tiree—Ionian serpentine marble. Wrenched from the seabed or shore by ice, the white, yellow, and green variegated fragments are polished like gemstones in the milling surf.

Sand, Peat, and Diatomite

The last stage in the physical creation of the geological mosaic has occurred in the last 10,000 years during which the hard rocky islands have been dressed in aeolian sand and peat, and, during a warm climatic period, deposits of diatomite have been laid in the beds of shallow lochs in Skye and Mull. The reduction of the crustal massif by erosion, which laid low the primeval mountains, was greatly accelerated by the ice ages of the late Pleistocene

to about 8,000 BP (before present). Since then the erosion
has continued, though on a greatly reduced scale.

The torrential streams of the denuded islands have
outwashed fans of sands and gravels which have built up
in the post-glacial period and, in the littoral, these are
continuously reworked into new shapes by spate and tide.
Hebridean streams now bear little silt even in times of
spate, but the slow, inexorable erosion of coastal rocks by
the sea continues. In Lewis (Broad Bay), Rum, Eigg,
Skye, Mull, Colonsay and Islay where friable sedimentary
and volcanic rocks are beaten by sand-laden waves, there
are drifts of rock sands and gravels. Among the most
famous of those rock sands are the 'Singing Sands' at the
Bay of Laig on Eigg, the black sands of Carsaig on the
Ross of Mull and the green olivine sands of Duntulm in
north Skye.

The origin of much of the sand on the Hebrides is not
in the solid crust of the earth, but in the sea. Over the
past 10,000 years in the post-glacial period (Halocene), the
seas of the Hebridean shelf have been highly productive
in marine life. The sea-shore, thousands of kilometres in
length, has been a ribbon of life, and each square metre
has been the living space of a community of marine
creatures, many of which lived only for a few years and
left hard shells and skeletons to be milled by the
breakers—barnacles, crabs, limpets, whelks, periwinkles,
bivalves, tube-worms, starfish, urchins and coralline
seaweeds.

Over thousands of years, the remains of this enormous
and continuous regeneration of life, mainly in the form of
crushed sea-shell, composed mainly of calcium carbonate,
came to dominate the western coasts of the Outer
Hebrides, Tiree and Coll. Brought by the sea to the shore
and made into sand, the wind then took over, and the
sand was blown inland to form dunes and machair plains.
Ultimately, in the interior of the islands, the calcareous
sand was blown over the indigenous peat, which had also
been developing over the hard core of the islands since
the disappearance of the ice. This mixture of shell-sand
and peat made a light fertile loam giving a basis for
agriculture and richness of wildlife.

While the sea was spreading its beneficence upon the
islands, another tryst was being struck between the land
and the atmosphere in the growth of vegetation in a
regime of temperature and humidity conducive to the
formation of peat. For around 1,000 years about 11,000
years BP, there was a re-advance of ice, before its final

retreat began about 10,000 years BP. There followed a rapid amelioration of the climate, and the spread of forest over the mainland and into the islands. This lasted for about 3,000 years, after which the climate became wetter, producing ideal conditions for the formation of peat, and with the exception of a drier period of a thousand years about 4,000 years BP, the wet conditions have continued until the present.

The layered peat contains the preserved pollen of the several climatic periods of post-glacial times, and the analysis of the pollen provides us with a record of the vegetation, particularly the advance of heath and forest from the south, in the aftermath of the northward retreating ice-sheet. Within this stratification of biotic material, there occurs deposits of diatomite, which is opaline silica of fine grain formed from the frustules of freshwater diatoms. There are six sites mostly associated with shallow lochs in Trotternish, Skye and some of these have a covering of peat over 3 m thick.

The Hebrides are characterised by their dark peaty landscapes away from the sand-blown Atlantic fringe. Blanket mires cover most of the interiors of the larger islands, and are most extensive in Lewis, Skye, Mull, Jura and Islay. The classical example of Holocene peat formation comes from the henge at Callanish in Lewis, where the megaliths were excavated in the 19th Century from 5 m of peat.

Islands and Geology

There cannot be a complete understanding of nature without a knowledge of the rocks, and of how they came to be as they are. The natural history of the Hebrides is founded on solid rock and drifting sediments, at the mercy of sea, streams, rain, sunshine and frost. The scenery, the climate, habitat, flora, fauna and people are all, in varying ways and degrees, dependent on rocks which form a basis for life. Great events in the tectonic history of the North Atlantic are writ upon the rocks of the Hebrides, as is the *raison d'etre* of plants and animals all in their proper living quarters, and of the physical and spiritual nature of human life. The rocks were there before life, and will remain after life is past.

Island-going is an adventure in learning. Discovery leads to wonder. Wonder is the evocation of natural beauty. Beauty is the imperative of love. The Hebrides, serene on the edge of the world between ocean and

continent, have been beloved of men and women over
seven thousand years. This thought came to JMB's mind
one day in Rum where, alone, he rested upon the dry
sand of a summer's day on the strand at Kilmory. He ran
the sand through his fingers and later wrote:

'Here in my hands', I mused, 'I hold the keys of Creation!'
With my index finger I spread the grains across my palm. I
saw each grain as a unique micro-entity in itself. 'But these are
the sands of time, not just of the past, but of the present and
the future', I exclaimed aloud, and my mind was gripped in a
rare Thoreauesque moment of truth.

As in the clearing of mist, I saw the origin and destiny of
the sand, and with it the whole planet. I saw the fire which
forged the crystals in the primeval crust, the igneous mountains
(now long vanished) beyond the record of geological time
which, through erosion, created the Torridonian sandstones of
Rum, Skye and Wester Ross. Raising my eyes by way of
confirmation that my vision was indeed real, I saw the eroding
Torridonian sandstone on Mullach Mor, from whence came the
sand in my hand. As I let it run through my fingers again and
again, I knew that no power on earth could arrest its eternal
journey to the rocks of the future.

> N'er saw I a sight so plain!
> A smudge of cold, brown sand
> Across the warmth of cuppéd hand,
> A moment did my mind entrain.
>
> 'But this', quoth I, 'is Torridonian
> In whose each high-piled band
> Dwells the spirit of an ancient land;
> Once great, now gone, ne'er to be again'.
>
> These grains, the Rock of Ages, sprang
> From the primeval, lifeless crust
> When no flower bloomed, and no bird sang.
>
> Upon this smudge for me did history hang
> The hour-glass of the ages, and entrust
> The Sands of Time to our safe keeping.

J. M. Boyd

We reflect upon this poignant moment to show what
meaning and wonder can be obtained from a simple,
mundane, encounter with grains of sand, and of how
much greater is the sense of wonder which awaits those
who thirst after, and reflect upon, the geology of these
islands!

The Seabird Islands

Seabirds are part of the very fabric of the Hebrides; the call of the sea-mew is heard in the lore and music of the Gaelic people, and that of the kittiwake can be heard in Mendelssohn's *Fingal's Cave*. In their cliff-bound home or over the awesome spaces of ocean, their natural gifts of flight are not only amazing in the physical sense, but also very beautiful, sometimes humorous and occasionally bizarre.

The west coast of Scotland has long been famous for possessing one of the richest seabird communities in the world. This reputation is based on accounts of a limited number of spectacular but remote breeding stations during the summer. Recent counts suggest that there are roughly a million breeding pairs, about a third of the total for Britain and Ireland, a tenth of that of western Europe and a twentieth of that of the cooler part of the Atlantic and adjacent seas.

Thus begins a key paper by Bourne and Harris (1979) to which this chapter largely refers, and provides a review of the literature from Harvie-Brown and Buckley (1888; 1892) to 'Operation Seafarer' (Cramp *et al.* 1974) and the ornithological atlas (Sharrock, 1974). Since then Thom (1986) has brought the records up-to-date in *Birds in Scotland*, and a Seabird Colony Register is in preparation by the Seabird Group of NCC.

There can be no full understanding of seabirds without first having a knowledge of climate and hydrography and of the ecology of the sea, the seashore and the coasts, and this we have covered in previous chapters. There are essentially three types of seabird according to feeding habits: firstly, the coastal species such as the gulls, cormorants and terns, some of which lead a semi-terrestrial life, frequent freshwaters and feed at sea within a few kilometres of the shore; secondly, the off-shore species such as auks, kittiwakes, skuas and gannets, which have a marine existence (except for breeding sites); thirdly, the

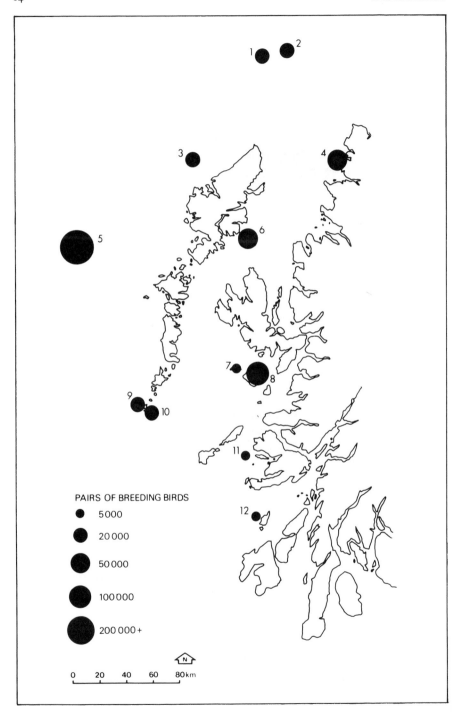

PAIRS OF BREEDING BIRDS

● 5000

● 20000

● 50000

● 100000

● 200000+

0 20 40 60 80km

Stac an Armin (190m) viewed from the summit of Boreray (380m), St Kilda holds about 12,000 pairs of gannets on its spire (Photo J. M. Boyd)

pelagic species such as the petrels which range widely from inshore waters to the vast expanses of ocean many hundreds of miles from land. Exceptions to this are the kittiwake (*Rissa tridactyla*) which is off-shore and oceanic in habit while all the other gulls range off-shore but are mainly coastal; the black guillemot (*Cepphus grylle*), which is coastal while all the other auks are off-shore; and the red-neck phalarope (*Phalaropus lobatus*), which is for most of the year a pelagic species ranging the oceans far from land, yet it breeds and raises its young in coastal freshwater habitats.

The Hebrides provide ideal seabird breeding habitat. Remote and varied coastlines lie within easy reach of feeding grounds at sea, the superlative cliffs of St Kilda heading a list of

Fig. 1
Map of the main seabird islands of the Hebrides. 1 Sula Sgeir, 2 North Rona, 3 Flannans, 4 Handa, 5 St Kilda, 6 Shiants, 7 Canna, 8 Rum, 9 Mingulay, 10 Berneray, 11 Treshnish, 12 Colonsay

first-class habitats for vertical cliff-nesting species such as kittiwakes, guillimots and shags, among which Mingulay and Berneray in the Barra Isles, the Shiant Isles and Handa in Sutherland are most notable. St Kilda also has spacious cliff terraces with much talus, and similar cliffs are also found in the Shiants and Treshnish Isles, affording nesting spaces for borrow- and crevice-nesting species such as puffins, Manx shearwaters, storm petrels, (Leach's Petrels also at St Kilda, Flannan Isles, North Rona and Sula Sgeir), razorbills and black guillimots. There is enormous scope for surface-nesting gulls and terns throughout the Hebrides, but gannets which may be ledge- or terrace-nesters are confined to large, long-established sites at St Kilda and Sula Sgeir, and small, recently-established colonies on the Flannans and Shiants. There is an almost endless set of options for breeding sites for all species of British seabird, yet so few of them are taken up, possibly because of poor food supply and predation.

The Islands

The seabird islands are shown in p. 14 and the distribution of species within them in Table 1.

Species Islands	fulmr p	manx s p	st pl	lh pl	gnnt p	corm p	shag p	ac sk p
North Rona	3738	0	pt	pt	0	0	126	0
Sula Sgeir	6532 i	0	pt	pt	9143	0	10	0
Flannan Islands	4734	0	pt	pt	414	0	336	0
St Kilda	62786	pt	pt	pt	50050	0	52	0
Lewis & Harris	16407	0	0	0	0	47	1368	48
Uists & Benbecula	1055	0	pt	0	0	105	55	6
Monach Islands	593	0	0	0	0	13	25	0
Barra *	486	0	0	0	0	0	0	0
Ming'y & Berneray	10457	0	pt	0	0	0	721	0
Shiant Islands	6816	0	0	0	1	? 0	1777	0
Skye & outliers #	3730	?	?	0	0	76	1677	0
Rum	581	116000	0	0	0	0	14	0
Canna Eigg Muck	1078	1085	0	0	0	0	1815	0
Coll Tiree Gunna	1510	0	0	0	0	1	140	47
Mull & outliers @	1773	pt	pt	0	0	42	578	0
Jura & outliers X	87	0	0	0	0	7	192	54
Colonsay & Oronsay	869	0	0	0	0	0	118	0
Islay	1469	0	0	0	0	0	393	0
Gigha & Cara	117	0	0	0	0	0	247	0
Summer Isles	1008	0	pt	0	0	0	108	0
Handa	3474	0	0	0	0	0	256	30

	gt sk p	bh gl p	cm gl p	lbb gl p	hg gl p	gbb gl p	kwe p	sh tn p
North Rona	14	0	0	2	80	733	3943	0
Sula Sgeir	0	0	0	0	13	3	1031	0
Flannan Islands	0	0	0	4	11	168	2779	0
St Kilda	54	0	0	154	59	56	7829	0
Lewis & Harris	36	140	292	260	1776	1258	2430	0

	gt sk p	bh gl p	cm gl p	lbb gl p	hg gl p	gbb gl p	kwe p	sh tn p
Uists & Benbecula	0	153	85	7	487	64	0	0
Monach Islands	0	57	61	10	78	52	0	0
Barra *	0	0	41	0	176	20	0	0
Ming'y & Berneray	6	0	2	94	405	170	8614	0
Shiant Islands	6	0	0	51	164	127	1864	0
Skye & outliers #	0	24	235	518	2896	344	1914	0
Rum	0	0	15	80	379	50	2213	0
Canna Eigg Muck	0	0	139	86	2142	160	1057	0
Coll Tiree Gunna	0	817	344	225	2899	267	1060	0
Mull & outliers @	0	2	276	80	2921	526	337	0
Jura & outliers X	0	197	280	931	2183	114	17	0
Colonsay & Oronsay	0	63	67	27	933	38	5646	0
Islay	0	17	361	407	1520	93	563	0
Gigha & Cara	0	26	194	355	818	56	0	0
Summer Isles	0	0	7	7	299	109	0	0
Handa	66	0	6	2	54	31	10732	0

	re tn p	cn tn p	ac tn p	le tn p	glmt i	rzbl i	b glmt i	pffn i
North Rona	0	0	0	0	17104	1038	54	5500
Sula Sgeir	0	0	0	0	24746	580	?	500p
Flannan Islands	0	0	0	0	21926	3160	6+	4400
St Kilda	0	0	0	0	22705	3814	17	230501
Lewis & Harris	0	114	762	13	1238	853	2172	273
Uist & Benbecula	0	114	508	50	0	0	302	0
Monach Islands	0	92	122	26	0	0	292	0
Barra *	0	43	60	0	0	0	61	0
Ming'y & Berneray	0	0	0	0	30881	16893	12	3570p
Shiants	0	0	0	0	18380	10948	31	77000p
Skye & outliers #	0	110	1291	0	2494	1151	2967	367
Rum	0	0	0	0	3644	471	122+	50p
Canna Eigg Muck	0	26	284	0	6873	2273	272	1086
Coll Tiree Gunna	0	403	76	79	727	289	13	1
Mull & outliers @	0	785	224	0	4775	322	224	1068
Jura & outliers X	0	537	326	0	0	27	112	0
Colonsay & Oronsay	0	40	724	0	13541	1450	397	0
Islay	0	15	638	15	2522	1239	555	0
Gigha & Cara	0	15	32	0	30	17	177	4
Summer Isles	0	67	67	0	0	63	86	0
Handa	0	8	4	0	98686	16394	?	803

Table 1   Populations of seabirds in the Hebrides. Numbers of all species except the auks and the fulmars on Sula Sgeir are *breeding pairs*. All the auks are *individuals*, except for four colonies of puffins which are *breeding pairs*. i = individuals; p = pairs; pt = present; * = Pabbay to Eriskay; # = South Rona, Raasay, Scalpay, Pabbay, etc; @ = Treshnish Isles, Iona, Ulva, Staffa, etc; X = Scarba, Luing, Lunga, Shuna etc. Harris and Lewis are separated from the Uists and Benbecula by the main channel of the Sound of Harris. Fulmr = fulmar, s = shearwater, pl = petrel, st = storm, Lh = Leach's, gnnt = gannet, corm = cormorant, sk = skua, ac = arctic, gt = great, gl = gull, bh = black-headed, cn = common, lbb = lesser black-backed, hg = herring, gbb = greater black-backed, kwe = kittiwake, tn = tern, sh = sandwich, re = roseate, le = little, glmt = guillemot, rzbl = razorbill, pffn = puffin. [These data are from the Seabird Colony Register (Compiler: Dr Clare Lloyd) of the Nature Conservancy Council's Seabird Group. Many of the data from the remote outliers were provided by the Seabirds at Sea Team of NCC.]

St Kilda

In Chapter 7 we describe the seabirds of the St Kilda group of islands, which have contributed to the declaration of these islands as a World Heritage Site. Here, we place St Kilda in the context of the other seabird islands of the Hebrides. The largest seabird assembly in one island—including its outliers—occurs on Boreray in the St Kilda group. Boreray (384m) and its two gigantic stacks, Stac an Armin (196m) and Stac Lee (172m), hold the largest assembly of North Atlantic Gannets (*Sula bassana*) in the world. There is a total of 50,000 pairs, with 13,500 on Stac Lee and 11,900 on Stac an Armin (Murray and Wanless, 1986), and they also have major colonies of kittiwakes, guillemots, razorbills, puffins, fulmars, Manx shearwaters, storm petrels and Leach's petrels, bringing the total number of breeding seabirds to well over 100,000 pairs. The other islands have somewhat smaller totals and no breeding gannets. St Kilda as a whole, though, with 320,000 breeding pairs, probably possesses over one-third of all the seabirds breeding in the Hebrides and about 11% of those breeding in Britain and Ireland. Seventeen species of seabird, including eider (*Somateria mollissima*) and red-necked phalarope have bred at St Kilda this century—the largest list for any British seabird colony. To sail close to the perpendicular walls, massive rock bastions, dark sinister caves and spectacular arches and rock pillars, all echoing with the calls of a myriad of seabirds, is to behold one of the natural wonders of the British Isles. The more adventurous captains take their ship between Stac Lee and Boreray and at the point of transit the sky is full of gannets, to port are the overhanging flanks of the stack and to starboard the mighty west wall of Boreray which appears caught in a snow storm of kittiwakes and guillemots, the drama heightened by gannets in hundreds diving into the wake of the ship as the disturbance brings fish to the surface.

The Shiants

The Minches have good stocks of pelagic fish and the Shiants are placed in the midst of rich feeding grounds for off-shore species of seabird—hence the large colony of puffins (77,000 pairs) and good numbers of guillemots (9,000 pairs). This is St Kilda in miniature, but without the rarer pelagic species—the Manx shearwater and the two small petrels. Neither does it possess an established gannetry. In 1984 a single nest was built on Eilean Mhuire and in 1985–86 single nests were also built on Garbh Eilean, but breeding has not yet been proved. The puffins are largely housed in a large talus slope on Garbh Eilean which is reminiscent of the Carn Mor, the now famous puffin-shearwater-small petrel site at St Kilda. The Shiants possess a rare and wonderful atmosphere, and from the summits there is a fine panorama of islands and distant mountains. The little house on Eilean an Tigh has been the base for many school expeditions which go there to study the seabirds and the eco-system of a remote island.

North Rona and Sula Sgeir

The Flannan Islands, Sula Sgeir, North Rona, Mingulay and Berneray all hold about the same number of breeding seabirds, between 24,000 pairs (Sula Sgeir) and 31,000 pairs (North Rona), and any one of those hold more than the rest of the Outer Hebrides (22,000 pairs). This is because of their consistently high stocks of guillemots, of an order similar to St Kilda (24,000 pairs) (Bourne and Harris, 1979). Sula Sgeir is but a rocky ridge 750m long and 250m wide, and every part of it seems tenanted. There are probably 13 species, and a remarkably sharp boundary exists between the tightly packed gannet grounds and guillemot stances and the open pattern of the fulmar grounds, with each sitting bird beyond 'spitting distance' of its neighbour. The stench of bird manure, rotting fish and fulmar oil is everywhere and the wild calling of thousands of piscivorous throats is deafening.

In the midst of this melee stand the low, dry-stone bothies of the gannet-hunters from Ness in Lewis, who come to the rock annually to take 2,000 *gugas* (young, unfledged gannets) to salt as food for the local people. This harvest of *gugas* is taken under licence; elsewhere in Britain the gannet is fully protected. In 1985, Stuart Murray counted 9,100 occupied nests of gannets on Sula Sgeir, and despite the off-take of over 20% of the young and the construction of a small lighthouse and helipad on the rock by the Northern Lighthouse Board, numbers seem to be steady at about 9,000 pairs. Murray noted that though the area on which the helipad now stands was not occupied by gannets when it was built in the early eighties, there were some 68 nests there in 1985!

North Rona has 13 species of breeding seabird. It is a major site for the guillemot (*c.* 2,000 pairs), storm petrel (order 3) and Leach's petrel (order 3). The 80 pairs of Arctic terns on the perched storm-beach on Fianuis are unusual for the distant outliers, and the colony of 730 pairs of great black-backed gulls is the largest in Britain. It is also a wonder that over 2,500 pairs of puffins—preferred prey for these gulls—have survived on this small 130ha. island.

The first account of the colonies of small petrels was by Ainslie and Atkinson (1937) and they were graphically described by Fraser Darling (1939) and Robert Atkinson (1949). Atkinson's youthful adventure in hitching a lift in a Stornoway drifter to North Rona and making some absolutely new discoveries in the biology of these little, exceedingly wild and remote species caught the imagination of young island-going naturalists who succeeded them in the exploration of the outliers of the British Isles. It is a wonderful experience to stand in the ruins of the Rona village—or the *cleitean* on Boreray—through the three dark hours of a June night and witness the arrival of the small petrels at their nests. Both ground and sky are alive with darting forms and the swish of wings; the soft, rhythmic purring and crooning of the stormies in their burrows ends in a distinct *hiccough*, while the Leach's in their bounding flight have a whirring call ending in a loud *wicka, wicka*.

Mingulay and Berneray

Mingulay and Berneray each have nine species of breeding seabird. Barra Head, which is another name for Berneray, is the most southerly point in the Outer Hebrides round which a sea-current flows from the Sea of the Hebrides. This current of in-shore water meets the westerly movement of ocean water south-west of Barra Head, and on this 'front' there is a rich food supply for seabirds. It is to be expected, therefore, that the southern isles of Barra should hold good breeding stocks of off-shore species, and accordingly there are 8,600 pairs of kittiwakes, 8,500 of razorbills and 15,500 of guillemots on Berneray and Mingulay. There are few puffins (3,600 pairs) compared with the Shiants (77,000), which are situated close to the largest concentrations in the Hebrides of Norway pout (*Trisopterus esmarkii*), a favourite food of puffins.

Small Isles

The major seabird island of the Inner Hebrides is Rum, which comes second to St Kilda in order of magnitude. However, Rum is greatly different in character to St Kilda since it owes its eminence to a single species—of the 120,000 pairs of 12 species of seabirds breeding on Rum (Wormell, 1976), 116,000 are

Manx shearwaters, nesting high on the mountain tops and hidden in burrows during hours of daylight. They emerge from and visit their burrows at night with a great cacophony of screeching, crowing and crooning from both the air and the ground. The Norsemen named one of the peaks tenanted by the shearwaters 'Trolaval', after the goblins who called so strangely in the night. (The survey of this vast shearwater 'conurbation' across the Rum cuillin is described in Chapter 6.) Otherwise Rum holds few other seabirds for its size—about 1,800 pairs of guillemots, 1,100 kittiwakes, 500 each of razorbills, fulmars and herring gulls and six other species with less than 100 pairs (Table 1).

Canna, Eigg and Muck also hold small populations of Manx shearwaters; Canna has about 1,000 pairs. During the day large numbers of shearwaters can be seen from the ferries around the Small Isles, Coll and Tiree, and on summer evenings large 'rafts' are present in the Sound of Rum, awaiting nightfall and subsequent flight to nesting grounds on the high tops. Canna may have storm petrels, and has the largest colonies of shags (1,000 pairs) and herring gulls (2,100 pairs) in the Hebrides.

Treshnish Isles and Others

The Treshnish Isles hold 14 species (Table 1) including three pelagic species—fulmar, Manx shearwater and storm petrel. There are also about 2,000 pairs of guillemots and 500 of puffins. A visit to the Treshnish Isles and Staffa on a bright, warm June day is glorious to the naturalist. The setting of seabirds on the pillared basalt walls, green-mantled terraces and among cushions of sea-pinks is idyllic, very different from the awesome seabird-thronged abysses of St Kilda, Mingulay and Handa. Colonsay and Oronsay have colonies of kittiwakes (5,600 pairs) and guillemots (6,500 pairs), while Tiree has small colonies of fulmars, shags, 6 species of gull, 3 species of tern, razorbill, guillemot and black guillemot. Coll has no cliff-nesting seabirds, but holds a small colony of Arctic skuas.

Handa

Handa is not strictly in the Hebrides, but the seabirds that breed there feed in Hebridean waters. The vertical galleried sandstone walls of Handa are ideal for guillemots, of which there are 50,000 pairs, and to a lesser extent razorbills (8,200 pairs) and kittiwake (5,300 pairs), but not for puffins (400 pairs). The concourse of guillemots nests close to large stocks of herring, mackerel, sprat and Norway pout (Bailey *et al.*) in the north Minch.

The large islands of Lewis and Harris, the Uists and Benbecula, Barra, Skye, Mull, Islay and Jura all possess small straggling colonies, though there are many hundreds of miles of coastline bereft of any breeding seabirds. For example, the north coast of Skye with the Ascarib Isles in Loch Snizort and the Rhinns of Islay both face 'fronts' with good supplies of fish and have many small colonies, but on the other hand the east coasts of both the Outer and Inner Hebrides possess very few breeding seabirds.

The Species

Fulmar

The stronghold of the fulmar is St Kilda, where there are 62,800 pairs. It is thought that it has nested there for over 800 years (Fisher, 1966) and has only come to occupy most of the coasts of Britain and Ireland in the last century. The spread is believed to have stemmed not from St Kilda, but from a genetically distinct race which colonised Foula from Iceland and Faeroe in 1878. One theory is that the Icelandic race has the ability to breed in small groups or isolated pairs, while the St Kilda race requires the local stimulation of large, dense assemblies for successful breeding. Another theory connects the spread with the warming of the North Atlantic over the last hundred years, and another with the spread of offal from the whaling (at the turn of the century in Shetland and Harris) and the fishing industries attracting fulmars into areas hitherto unoccupied by them. In truth, no one knows. In the Hebrides it is not quite ubiquitous, not breeding on much of the east coast of Harris and North Uist, the west coast of South Uist and all of Benbecula, the east and south coasts of Skye from Staffin to Loch Scavaig, on South Rona and Raasay, the east coast of Mull from Ardmore Point to Carsaig, Lismore and the isles in the Firth of Lorne, Jura and East Islay from Bunnahabhain to Port Ellen (Thom, 1986). Why such long stretches of the coast should remain unoccupied is a mystery, though the fulmar seems much less attracted to sheltered than to exposed coasts. It is particularly numerous in highly exposed isles with adjacent, rich, turbulent seas, such as St Kilda, Mingulay, North Rona, Sula Sgeir, Shiants and Handa.

Professor G. M. Dunnet and colleagues (1978, 1979, 1982), working on Eynhallow in Orkney, showed that fulmars are about ten years old before they breed, by which time only about 6% return to the native colony. The survival rate for adults is about 97%, which shows the great hardiness of this inhabitant of the tempestuous coasts.

Manx Shearwater

The Manx shearwater is one of the most numerous seabirds in the Hebrides; more numerous than the fulmar, gannet, herring gull, kittiwake and razorbill, but less so than the guillemot and much less than the puffin. Yet shearwaters are an uncommon sight in most of the Hebrides. It is known that the birds disperse widely to distances of up to 200km from nest sites in foraging flights, and increase in numbers within 10km of breeding islands during the late afternoon and into the evening, when large 'rafts' of often over a thousand birds form off-shore on the sea's surface, awaiting nightfall.

The major colonies are on Rum and St Kilda, with smaller centres on Canna (Swann in Campbell, 1984), Eigg, Muck (Dobson, 1985), Treshnish Isles, and at Gallan Head in Lewis.

A Manx shearwater caught in the lap of a night visitor to Carn Mor, St Kilda (Photo J. M. Boyd)

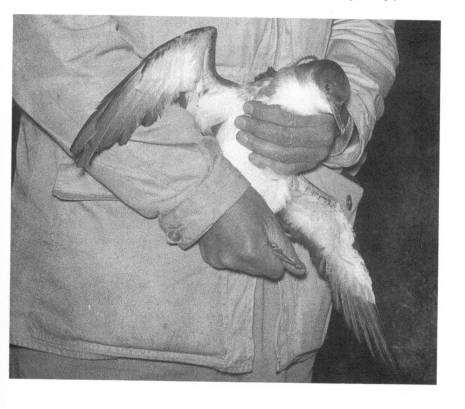

Shearwaters are, therefore, most numerous in the Sea of the Hebrides, and can be seen from ferries serving the islands from Oban and Mallaig, their dark shapes and swerving, gliding, skimming flights are unmistakable compared with the straight missile-like trajectory of the auks. The passage to St Kilda also features the shearwaters in great numbers, and the sooty shearwater (*Puffinus griseus*) and great shearwater (*Puffinus gravis*), both of which breed in the South Atlantic, are seen occasionally around St Kilda. Cory's shearwater, which breeds in the Mediterranean and from Azores to the Cape Verde Islands, has been seen off Islay, North Uist and Lewis, and the little shearwater (*Puffinus assimilis*) was seen off Islay on 30th June 1974. Rings on Manx shearwaters breeding in Scotland have been recovered from South American waters and the Gulf of Mexico—a juvenile was found off Argentina, 9,830km from its nest site eight weeks after the ring was fixed.

A midnight visit to the summits of Hallival and Askival on Rum, or Carn Mor on St Kilda to hear the home-coming of the shearwater host is an exciting experience. Their weird haunting call comes in surges upon the wind; the incoming birds arriving with rising shrieks of *kukroo-kukroo-kukroo*, ending with the strike of the bird at the burrow and sometimes on the lap of the observer. They are wild and vicious, and their barbed beaks will tear unwary hands.

Small Petrels

The storm petrel breeds at nine sites between Sanda and North Rona, and it is also a widespread breeder in Orkney and Shetland (Thom, 1986)—breeding is suspected at six other sites. Only two colonies are thought to exceed 100 pairs: St Kilda (>10,000 pairs) and Priest Island, Summer Isles (*c.* 10,000). The only other large colony in Scotland is on Foula (1,000–10,000). However, the actual numbers present at all sites are largely unknown. Breeding probably occurs on the outliers on the west of the Outer Hebrides from Monach to Loch Roag and in the Sound of Harris—we heard one calling from a burrow at Shillay, Harris in September 1953. Also, breeding is suspected on Canna and the Shiants. They are unlikely to be found on islands possessing rats, and ringed birds show that many colonies may be visited by young birds before they settle to breed. In summer, birds ringed in Scotland have been caught in Norway, Faeroe and Iceland and in winter, off the African coast from Liberia to Natal.

Leach's petrel breeds at St Kilda, Flannans, North Rona and Sula Sgeir; the only other breeding records in Britain and

Ireland are in recently established sites at Foula (1974) and Ramna Stacks (1980). Both species of small petrel have a protracted breeding season—we have heard them at Carn Mor in April and at North Rona in October. The single white egg is usually incubated from early June and the last young go to sea in November. Until 1955, knowledge of small petrels was confined to the works of Atkinson and Ainslie (1937), and Darling (1940) referring to North Rona. Possibly the largest colony in Britain which contains both species of small petrel is on Carn Mor, Dun and Boreray at St Kilda (Boyd, Tewnion and Wallace, 1956). The difficulties of measuring the size of such colonies are formidable, yet the assembly of Leach's at St Kilda can be reliably assessed in thousands, in hundreds on the Flannans, North Rona and Sula Sgeir, and in tens at other sites. There are single old records of Wilson's Petrel (*Oceanites oceanicus*) from June (1891), and the white-faced petrel (*Pelagodroma marina*) from Colonsay (1897).

Gannet

Wanless (1986) estimated a world population of gannets occupying 263,200 nest sites (pairs), of which 223,400—85%—are in the East Atlantic, and Scotland has 131,800, 59% of which are at 12 sites. St Kilda alone has 50,100 nest sites, and the Hebrides as a whole has 59,220 nest sites. There are three Gannetries: St Kilda, Sula Sgeir (9,100), Flannans (410) (Table 1, and p. 15); however, gannets from Ailsa Craig (21,500) and Sule Stack (4,000) fish in the Hebrides. They do no overfly isthmuses, so there are daily passages mainly of St Kilda birds round the Butt of Lewis, through the sounds of the Outer Hebrides to and from the feeding grounds in the Minches and the Sea of the Hebrides. In like manner birds from Ailsa Craig fly round the Mull of Kintyre and through the Sounds of Islay and Gunna to the Sea of the Hebrides and beyond.

The gannet usually feeds by plummeting from a height of 20 to 30m into the sea, catching its prey on the dive and usually swallowing the fish before it surfaces. It feeds mostly on pelagic fish—mackerel, herring, sprat—which are most plentiful in the Minches and the Sea of the Hebrides (Bailey *et al.*, 1979). There are also feeding grounds around St Kilda where shoals of mackerel and sand-eels break the surface of Village Bay on calm mid-summer evenings. In winter Scottish breeding gannets move south, mostly to the Bay of Biscay, but some reach tropical West African water and others enter the Mediterranean. In January they head northward again, returning to the breeding islands in February and March in preparation for egg-laying in April, though some stay in British waters all winter.

The gannet has been increasing in numbers during this century, maybe as a result of a relaxation in hunting, though the colonies which are still harvested in the Vestmannaeyjar group in Iceland, Mykinesholmur in Faeroe, and Sula Sgeir are stable or increasing in numbers. New colonies are forming, even though the ability of the gannet to establish new colonies may be limited by social factors. It is thought (Nelson, 1978) that until a threshold of pairs — 20–35 — has been established, there is insufficient social stimulation for successful breeding. However, when this threshold has been reached, as it now has in the Flannans though not in the Shiants, the colonies increase rapidly. It is also known that young gannets may not return to their birth colony when they settle to breed. The steady state of the Sula Sgeir colony points to this, and ringed birds from the Bass Rock and Ailsa Craig (the only substantial ringing-sites for gannets in Scotland) have been found in Icelandic and Norwegian colonies.

Cormorant and Shag

The cormorant is distinguished from the shag by its larger size, heavy bill, white cheeks and chin, white thigh patches in breeding birds, and white breast in the immature birds. It lacks the crest possessed by the breeding shag, and is a much rarer bird than the shag in Britain. The cormorant is limited as a breeder to a few well-separated sites while the shag is wide-spread as a breeder in many sites, and almost ubiquitous as a fish-hunter in the Hebrides. Whereas the cormorant breeds on open sites with full exposure to the elements, the shag nests in caves, overhung cliff-bottoms, and in crevices under boulders on cliff-terraces immediately above the sea. The cormorant feeds mostly on bottom-feeding fish in shallow water and freshwaters, while the shag feeds on fish in the water column, and almost exclusively at sea.

There is a regal look to the cormorant as it stands tall in its rookery. The shag on the other hand, looks sinister and almost bizarre, as it perches erect in the Stygian gloom of its sea cave, merging with dark rock and shadow. However, when the shag emerges into the sunshine, it displays the finest vestments; its iridescent dark-green and black plumage has the sheen of silk. Both species are known as *scarbh* (scarv) in Gaelic.

In the Outer Hebrides, the cormorant has two main breeding sites; at Loch an Tomain (*c.* 100 pairs), a freshwater loch in North Uist, and on Stockay (*c.* 13 pairs) in the Monach Isles. Other small colonies exist in Loch Roag, Lewis, and in South Uist and Barra. Bourne and Harris (1979) stated that *c.* 380 occupied nests can occur in the Outer Hebrides, Thom (1986) stated that there are 240 pairs in West Inverness and Argyll. Most of these are in the Inner Hebrides scattered in small groups on the west coast of Skye, Rum, Ross of Mull and Mull of Kintyre. In Tiree cormorants have recently used Ceann a'Mhara as a perching site, and they are frequently seen at sea and on the freshwater lochs. About 16% of the Scottish population breed in the Hebrides. In winter, cormorants disperse in coastwise movements to other sectors of the British and Irish coasts, but a few from Scotland reach points ranging from Spain to Norway.

In contrast to the patchy occurrence of the cormorant, the shag is present on the bird islands usually in tens, occasionally in hundreds, and in Canna there are four large and many small breeding colonies with about 1,000 pairs in total. Numbers fluctuate greatly from year to year and in Canna counts in 1970 and 1971 were 200 and 1,900 pairs respectively, but 800–900 is a recent average size (Swann in Campbell, 1984). Only about 100 birds remain around Canna in winter, and ring returns show that the rest disperse throughout the Hebrides, mostly to the Outer Isles. Of all shags ringed, 70% have been recovered within 100km of the site of ringing; only 1% of Scottish rings have been recovered from France and Norway. The *scarbh* is still shot illegally for food in the Hebrides and often dies in fishing nets.

Skuas

The skuas are uncommon in the Hebrides in comparison with Orkney and Shetland; they are boreal species breeding on a NE-SW front of declining numbers from Unst, Shetland, to Jura. The great skua or 'bonxie' has extended its breeding range SW in the last 30 years and now breeds in North Rona (14 pairs), Lewis (*c.* 30 at 3 sites), St Kilda (54), Mingulay (6), and Handa (66), and there have been recent records of breeding on the Shiants and the Summer Isles. The Arctic skua breeds in small groups of up to 20 pairs in the moorlands of Lewis, North Uist, Benbecula, Coll and Jura. The dark phase predominates, and pairs are occasionally of dark and light birds.

The skuas are pirates, chasing gulls, gannets, terns and auks to a point when the hapless victim disgorges the contents of its crop, upon which the skua swiftly stoops. They are also preda-tors of other seabirds, killing adults and pillaging eggs and nestlings. The bonxie can kill a bird as large as a gannet, and is the boldest of birds in defending its own nest-site against an intruder sheep and sheep dogs can be harried and cowed by the diving bonxies and chased from the nesting area. Nearby, there are usually pools at which the bonxies bathe, preen, and stand with raised wings, cackling. They rise to meet the intruder barking loudly and then suddenly swoop in attack, sometimes striking the head with their feet before climbing away with a guttural *tuk-tuk-tuk*. Though the birds are unlikely to cause injury to a person, the onslaught takes nerve to resist, and usually results in a hasty, head-down retreat. In the Northern Isles the two species often nest on the same ground, and on Noss in Shetland the nesting area of the bonxie is extending at the expense of the arctic skua. Such competition may also occur in the nesting areas north of Gress in Lewis. The young of both species are great wanderers; ring returns from Scottish great skuas range from Greenland and Spitzbergen to the Mediterranean, Cape Verde Islands and the coasts of New England and Brazil, and ring returns from Arctic skuas are similarly well distributed, but there is a concerted movement to the Mediterranean and West Africa as far south as Angola in winter. Over 100 (presumably immature birds) have been seen off North Uist in May.

The Pomarine skua (*Stercorarius pomarinus*) is an oceanic species which breeds in arctic USSR, winters in the tropical Atlantic, and occurs on spring passage in the Outer Hebrides in flocks ranging from a few birds to over 1000. The long-tailed skua (*Stercorarius longicaudus*) nests in the Scandinavian arctic, and also occurs in spring passage in the Outer Hebrides, where, off Balranald in North Uist, 271 were counted on a day in late May and 390 between 18th and 25th May 1983.

Gulls

The herring gull is the 'sea-gull' of common usage; its voice is the familiar reminder of the seaside to the urban dwellers, and its gliding flight in the slip-stream of the ship is the fascination of ferry passengers. However, its clamouring flocks at rubbish dumps and fishing stations and its foul disregard for buildings, vehicles and boats is the scourge of the burghers of Stornoway, Portree, Tobermory and Port Ellen. Herring gulls have been suspected of spreading disease, especially *Salmonella*, and contaminating domestic water supplies. There are *c.* 3,500 pairs of breeding herring gulls in the Outer Hebrides, of which *c.* 1,800 are in Lewis and Harris. Bourne and Harris (1979) estimated *c.* 1,800 occupied nests of herring gulls, *c.* 1,100 of lesser black-

backed gulls, 221 of great black-backed gulls and 27 of common gulls in 18 sites on the moors of Lewis.

Herring gulls and lesser black-backed gulls at Mallaig harbour (Photo J. M. Boyd)

The herring gull is a commensal species nesting within easy flying distance of human settlement where it is a scavenger. There are comparatively few herring gulls at the outlying stations of St Kilda (<100 pairs), Flannans (<30), North Rona (*c.* 80), Sula Sgeir (*c.* 13), though the Inner Hebrides are more densely occupied, with all the seabird islands holding over 100 pairs and Canna *c.* 800. The lesser black-back is less of a scavenger and seems more at home in the outliers. When St Kilda was first occupied by the army, the camp swill was dumped daily at the jetty in Village Bay to the accompaniment of a noisy cloud of gulls. Most of these were herring gulls with fewer lesser black-backs, single Iceland gulls (*Larus glaucoides*) and glaucous gulls (*Larus hyperboreus*). This did not however result in an increase in the size of the gull colonies. The lesser black-backs became established in the mid-fifties before the army arrived with a subsequent increase in their breeding in the 1970s but with little change in the herring gull.

In autumn, there is a south-easterly movement of herring gulls from the Hebrides to the conurbations of Strathclyde and the Moray Firth, with a return movement in spring. We have seen a wing-tabbed herring gull off Tiree in June which had been caught at the Bishopriggs rubbish dump in Glasgow in the previous winter. The lesser black-back is much less numerous than the herring gull. In the Outer Hebrides there are *c.* 500 pairs of lesser black-backs, a migratory species which overwinters in the western Mediterranean and West Africa. Lesser black-backs breeding in Faeroe and Iceland move through the Hebrides in large numbers in spring and autumn.

The great black-back, unlike other species of gull, does not nest in dense colonies, and where there are many nesting together such as on North Rona, the nests are usually well-separated. It seems to be much more sensitive to disturbance than the other species, and often nests in solitude on spacious moorland, remote headlands, surf-grit islets, the tops of stacks inaccessible to sheep and man, but within easy access to feeding grounds.

There are *c.* 2,600 pairs of great black-backs breeding in the Outer Hebrides, and North Rona is the headquarters, with *c.* 730 pairs. This is an astonishing number in such a small island (130 ha.) for a bird of solitary nesting habit. However, conditions are probably ideal—an uninhabited, seldom-visited island with sheep and good nesting colonies of kittiwakes and auks, 19km from the gannetry and auk colonies on Sula Sgeir and close to commercial fishing grounds. In Lewis the largest colony (125 pairs) is on Druim Mor facing Broad Bay. In the other islands the great black-back breeds in tens, with the largest assembly (*c.* 100 pairs) in the Inner Hebrides on the Treshnish Isles. After breeding, there are roosting flocks sometimes hundreds strong including many immatures, which disperse southward into Ireland and the British mainland in winter. Few go further.

The common gull (*Larus canus*) is far from 'common' in the Hebrides, where the Outer Hebrides are thought to have *c.* 600 pairs. It does not breed in the outliers, and breeds in tens in the Inner Hebrides. Even the large islands may not have more than 100 pairs. Tiree, a favourable island, has usually 50–100 pairs. In winter the birds disperse southwards to Ireland and lowland Scotland, where they are joined by others from many parts of Scotland to form flocks many thousands strong.

The black-headed gull (*Larus ridibundus*) breeds throughout the main chain of the Outer Hebrides, Tiree, Coll, Colonsay, Jura, Islay and Gigha, but not in the outliers, Skye, Raasay, the Small Isles and Mull. It is a highly gregarious species, which nests in close proximity to human settlement, feeding on agricultural land, the microcrustacea of the shore, domestic and fishery litter, and nesting in swampy fens and bogs. In the Outer Hebrides there are >400 pairs in well scattered sites throughout the islands, with the largest colony (>200 pairs) at Loch Stiapavat, Lewis. Tiree and Coll can have over 700 pairs in several colonies in good years, but here as elsewhere, the colonies are disturbed by visitors and at least one has been destroyed by drainage. In winter the black-head is moulted with only a dark ear spot remaining, and the birds disperse southward to Ireland and the British mainland providing recruits for the wintering flocks on the Clyde and Solway coasts.

The kittiwake (*Rissa tridactyla*) is a gull in a class of its own; it is an off-shore, oceanic feeder. The Hebrides hold some 42,000 breeding pairs, 18,500 in the Outer and 23,500 in the Inner Hebrides. The headquarters of the kittiwake is at Handa, St Kilda and Berneray, which both hold *c.* 9,000 pairs. Where they occur, they nest in thousands. However, in some of the Inner Hebrides they are in hundreds but very seldom in tens. It is this highly gregarious, dainty gull which enlivens the seabird islands with its snow-white plumage, delicate flight, spectacular nest site and musical chorus.

Counts at St Kilda and Ailsa Craig show that over the two decades from 1959–79 numbers fluctuated greatly. The reasons for this are complex, but probably related to the availability of sufficient food for chick survival over sustained periods of years. The immature kittiwake is particularly handsome, with a dark W across the outstretched wing, and a black tip to the tail. It spends two years at sea before returning to breed in the third year. During this time, and also in winter as adults, they wander great distances across the Atlantic and into the Mediterranean.

The Iceland gull (*Larus glaucoides*) and the glaucous gull (*L. hyperboreus*) are winter visitors, and occasionally present as immatures in summer; the little gull (*L. minutus*), Sabine's gull (*L. sabini*), the ring-billed gull (*Larus delawarensis*—first recorded in Scotland in South Uist, 1981), Ross's gull (*Rhodostethia rosea*) and the ivory gull (*Pagophila eburnea*) have been recorded recently as vagrants in the Hebrides.

Terns

The Arctic tern is by far the most numerous tern in Scotland, and about 65,000 pairs (90%), breed in Orkney and Shetland. By contrast, only about 5,000 pairs breed in the Hebrides, two-thirds of them in the Outer Hebrides. The colonies are short-lived. In Tiree the total number of arctic terns (*c.* 400 pairs) has probably not changed greatly over the past 30 years, yet they have changed greatly from year to year in any one locality. After an absence of many years, they suddenly settle to breed at an old breeding site, and will be gone in the following year or two. The largest concentrations are probably on the Monach Isles (900 pairs in 1979), Coll and Tiree (*c.* 400), Treshnish Isles (*c.* 300) and on the isolated islet of Heiskeir (Oigh-sgeir) off Canna.

The terns are elegant, slender birds of white and pale grey plumage with black heads and a delicate, pulsating flight. They fiercely defend their vulnerable nests and young against intruders; rats, cats, dogs, otters, mink, crows, gulls and man are vigorously attacked by the swooping, screeching birds. Flashing past the head, the tern jabs home its sharp bill, sometimes drawing blood. The little tern (*Sterna albifrons*) is, in our experience, the fiercest of all, but they have little defence against the persistent predator. When breeding, they feed mainly on sand-eels, and during the day the birds are absent from the colony, fishing at sea. The Scottish terns travel to the West African coast for the winter. Arctic terns travel far into the southern hemisphere; some were recorded off Natal in November having travelled 10,000km in four months.

The common tern is in fact, far less 'common' than the Arctic tern. In the Outer Hebrides there were thought to be about 750 pairs in 1980, and in the Inner Hebrides there are small colonies of usually less than 30 pairs in Tiree, Coll, Treshnish, Colonsay and Handa. However, there are probably more than meets the eye, since this species can very easily be mistaken for the Arctic tern from which it differs by having a black tip to its bill. As in Orkney, there are probably over 2,000 pairs in the Hebrides compared with over 11,000 in Shetland. The little tern breeds in many colonies of a few pairs throughout the length of the Outer Hebrides (90 pairs) particularly in the Monach Isles (26) and Eoligarry, Barra (12). The Inner Hebrides has similar small colonies in Tiree, Coll, Islay and Gigha. One pair of Sandwich Terns (*Sterna sandvicensis*) nested in the Monach Isles in 1978, but there is no other breeding record from the Outer or Inner Hebrides. Roseate terns (*Sterna dougallii*) have been sighted in both Inner and Outer Hebrides between May and July, and a pair was present at Balranald, North Uist in May 1969. The black tern (*Chlidonias niger*) and the white-winged black tern (*Chlidonias leucopterus*) have occurred in the Outer Hebrides as vagrants in June 1978 and May 1964 respectively.

Auks

These are the guillemots, razorbills and puffins which are adapted both for flying and for swimming penguin-like in pur-

*Puffin (Photo
J. M. Boyd)*

suit of their prey. They are splendid black (or sooty-brown) and
white, frock-coated birds, occupying the sea-cliffs and cliff-
terraces. They occur in great numbers and though highly gregarious at their nesting sites, disperse widely in small numbers
over a vast expanse of sea. Scotland holds 80 and 90%
respectively of the British and Irish populations of guillemots
and puffins. The observed occurrence of auks at sea in the
Hebrides in summer and winter is shown in Fig. 11.5 (Bourne
and Harris, 1979).

The stronghold of the guillemot (*Uria aalge*) is in the
Northern Isles (207,000 birds *not pairs*), and the Hebrides,
including Handa and the Mull of Kintyre (103,000). In the case
of the razorbill (*Alca torda*) and the puffin (*Fratercula arctica*) the
weightings are reversed (Cramp *et al*, 1974). However, in 1988
c. 270,000 guillemots were counted in the Hebrides (Table
1). The most important sites for auks are in the outliers, the
Shiants and Handa, but the weightings of the species at each
island are different depending on the proximity of feeding

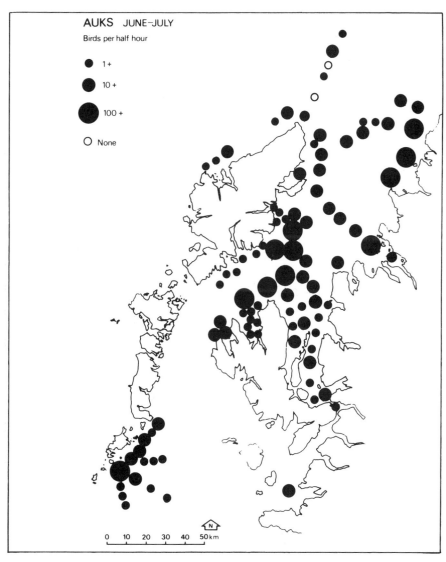

Fig. 2 *a & b*
*The seasonal
distribution of auks at
sea in the Hebrides
(from Bourne and
Harris, 1979)*

grounds and the nature of the cliff habitat. Let us compare
Handa and the Shiants. Both have similar feeding grounds in
the Minch, but they have a very different cliff ecology. The
former having horizontally stratified sandstone in vertical, galleried cliffs, ideal for guillemots and razorbills, but poor for
puffins, and the latter having vertically-jointed basalt with talus
and green terraces which, though only moderately favourable
for guillemots and razorbills, is ideal for puffins.

Guillemots nest on flat or slightly bevelled ledge systems,

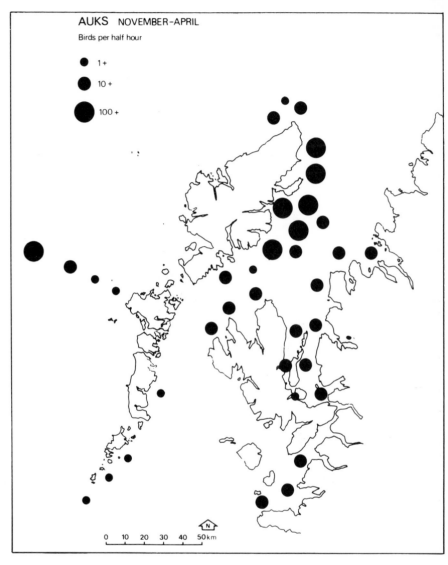

AUKS NOVEMBER–APRIL

Birds per half hour

and razorbills in clefts in cliffs, crevices under talus, and burrows. Their eggs are top-shaped so that when disturbed they do not roll from the ledge, but sit-up and spin on the spot. The puffin on the other hand is a burrow- and crevice-nester. It is seen at its densest on Dun, St Kilda, which is for the most part a single great puffin terrace.

There are three races of guillemot, two of which occur in the Scottish waters. *Uria aalge hyperborea* breeds in the Arctic and is a winter visitor; *U.a.aalge* the black northern race and *U.a.al-*

Guillemots (Photo J. MacGeoch)

bionis the sooty-brown, southern race breed in Scotland, the latter predominating in the Hebrides. There is also a north-south gradation of the 'bridled' form, which has a white eye-ring. In Shetland >20% are 'bridled', in the Hebrides >10% and in the south of England only 1%. The razorbill (*A. torda*) is of the race *islandica*, breeding from Iceland to Brittany, and the puffin (*F. arctica*) is of the race *grabae* breeding from the Faeroe Islands and southern Scandinavia to France.

Guillemots and razorbills have been increasing in numbers in recent years in Scotland, and this has been seen in Canna and Tiree. During the 1950s, the puffin population on Hirta, St Kilda declined and fringe colonies entirely disappeared while dense colonies became noticeably depleted (Harris, 1984). During this period, puffins may not have decreased in other islands of St Kilda which were densely stocked, and the species was increasing elsewhere in Scotland. After a period of stabilisation the population on Hirta is again increasing by about 4% per annum. Such fluctuations are probably related to a decline in the preferred food of the puffin in the established fishing areas, which is reflected in chick survival. In 1959, widespread mortality of puffin chicks occurred on Hirta; on Dun alone there were estimated to have been at least 8,000 dead, and autopsies showed death by starvation (Boddington, 1960).

Guillemots ringed in the Hebrides, mainly on Canna, have been found as juveniles in the North Sea, but adult recoveries have been mainly from southern England, with a few from France and Spain. Razorbills from the Hebrides do not appear in the North Sea, but probably move southward in company with the guillemots. Puffins disperse widely in all directions in winter; two chicks ringed on Sule Skerry on consecutive days were recovered in the following December as far apart as Newfoundland and Tenerife.

The black guillemot (*Cepphus grylle*) or 'tystie', is comparatively rare; the Scottish population was estimated as about 7,500 pairs in 1969–70, with 530 in the Outer Hebrides and possibly about 1,000 in the Hebrides as a whole. Recent counts on Skye and the Monach Isles indicate that these are substantial underestimates. In 1988, 7,900 birds were counted in the Hebrides, but the apparent increase may be related to a much more assiduous survey in recent years. Unlike the guillemot, which is concentrated in large, well separated breeding colonies, the 'tystie' is present on most islands in small nesting groups of seldom more than 10 pairs but sometimes, as at Shillay in the Monachs and Belnahua in Lorne, 20 or more. They disperse locally in autumn, acquiring their winter garb and seldom travelling more than 100km from the nest site. The little auk (*Alle alle*) is a winter vagrant in the Outer Hebrides and the extinct great auk (*Pinguinis impennis*) was last recorded at Stac an Armin, St Kilda in July 1840.

CHAPTER 3   **The Seal Islands**

Seals have great public appeal and are protected by popular acclaim, despite the complaints of fishermen and fish farmers about the damage they do to their trade. Remote, strange animals, they fascinate many people, and their apparent wide-eyed innocence strikes a chord of sympathy in the human mind. Fraser Darling wrote (1939):

the great seals are the people of the sea and it is not to be wondered at that Gaeldom should have invested them with half-veiled but occasionally irruptive humanity.

In Britain there are two species of seal: the grey seal (*Halichoerus grypus*) and the common seal (*Phoca vitulina*). The grey seal breeds in the Hebrides between September and November. Pupping occurs above highwater mark at traditional sites where bulls hold a kind of territory which can extend into the sea, but is more usually well above the shore. Mothers and pups stay ashore during nursing, but part when the mother is mated

Common seal (Photo J. M. Boyd)

at the end of the short nursing period. The common seal pups in June and July, and birth and nursing of pups takes place on inter-tidal sand and rock and in the sea. The grey seal pup may drown if it enters the sea before it is weaned and has moulted its thick, white, natal coat known as *lanugo*, whereas the common seal pup sheds its lanugo *in utero* and is born with its sea-going coat, so swims immediately with its mother.

The full-grown grey seals are distinctly larger than any common seals. The dark, broad forehead and large muzzle of the grey seal bull distinguish it from the grey seal cow, which has a steel-grey head and back, a shorter muzzle and cream-coloured blotching on the chest and belly, although some females can also be quite dark. The literal translation of the scientific name for the grey seal is the 'Roman-nosed sea pig', and this is probably a concise and apt description of the species. In the common seal there is less difference between the sexes, and both have shorter muzzles than greys with a smaller, more rounded head and body colour varying from dark brown to fawn, often spotted all over. There is an overlap in the appearance of the juvenile greys with adult commons, and the best diagnosis of species is in the arrangement of the nostrils: in the grey they are well-spaced ventrally, while in the common they are V-shaped. There is also a difference in the type of coastline that the two species inhabit. The grey seal likes exposed coasts and is at home around the outlying islands, while the common prefers sheltered coasts, and because of this is called the 'har-

Grey seal bull fresh from the sea in his breeding territory on the sheep-grazed pastures of Shillay, Sound of Harris in September 1953 (Photo J. Donaldson)

bour seal' in other parts of the world. In the Hebrides the grey seal is often found sharing sheltered waters with the common seal, but the common seal is very seldom seen in the surf-bound habitats of the grey seal, though it does occur in very exposed sites in Shetland and Tiree.

Seals and the Hebrideans

Ron Mor, the great seal, is part of Gaelic lore. The mysticism which surrounds the grey seal is described by Seton Gordon (1926):

> Among the people of the isles these great seals have always been regarded as half human. It is said that the clan MacCodrum had affinity with the seals, and at the annual seal battue in autumn an old woman of the clan was always seized by violent pains out of sympathy with her kinsfolk of the sea that were then being murdered in their surf-drenched home.

Today, with the decline of local fisheries and the statutory protection of seals, there is less contact between people and seals and the mystical traditions have faded. In historical times there was never a widespread tradition of seal hunting in the Hebrides, though the hunter-fishermen from mesolithic to medieval times probably hunted seals as the Scandinavians and Eskimos have always done. Seals provided meat, oil and hides for the islanders, but these commodities have been superseded in time by home-produced agricultural products, imported rubber and leather ware, fuel oils, bottled gas and pharmaceuticals. The first account of seal hunting in the Hebrides is by Martin (1703) in North Uist:

> On the Western Coast of this Island lyes the Rock Cousmil (Cousamul) . . . still famous for the yearly fishing of Seals there, in the end of October . . . the Parish Minister hath his choice of all the young Seals and that which he takes is called Cullen Mory, that is Virgin Mary's seal . . . When the crew are quietly landed, they surround the Passes, and then the signal for the general attacque is given from the Boat and so they beat them down with big staves . . . giving them many blows before they are killed . . . I was told also that 320 Seals, Young and Old, have been killed at one time in the Place.

During the height of the human population in the mid-19th century, after the collapse of the kelp industry when poverty and malnutrition were rife, seal hunting probably became a widespread necessity. In 1844, North Rona became uninhabited and the build-up of the large grey seal assembly there probably dates from that time (Boyd, 1963). By 1880, there were enough seals breeding on Rona to attract hunters, who also visited Sula Sgeir to take gannets (see p. 19). Similarly, when St Kilda was evacuated in 1930 and the Monach Isles in 1944, breeding colonies of grey seals became established, and we believe that the increase in the grey seal population in the Hebrides, recorded in the second half of this century, began in the middle of last century following the withdrawal of man from the outlying islands both as a resident and as a visiting seal-hunter. Since the Conservation of Seals Act, 1970, grey seals have been killed in the Hebrides to protect fisheries and fish farms and, under licence, to supply a small craft industry in seal skins which has now declined. In 1977, an unsuccessful attempt was made by the Department of Agriculture and Fisheries for Scotland to reduce substantially the number of seals breeding on Gasker and the Monach Isles by a licensed Norwegian sealer; 324 adult seals were killed but bad weather caused the operation to be abandoned.

Size and Distribution of the Grey Seal Population

The Sea Mammal Research Unit of the Natural Environment Research Council surveys the grey seals on their breeding grounds each year. The estimated number of grey seals in Great Britain in 1985 is given in Table 2.

Stock	Year	Pup production	Population size	Probable status
Inner Hebrides	1985	1,700	7,500	Unknown
Outer Hebrides (incl. N. Rona)	1985	10,900	42,500	Increasing
Orkney	1985	6,900	26,900	Increasing
Shetland	1983	1,000	3,500	Unknown
L. Eriboll & Helmsdale	1984	900	3,100	Unknown
Farne Isles	1985	860	4,400	Stable*
Isle of May	1985	800	4,000	Stable*
SW Britain	1982	850	3,000	Unknown

* These stocks are shown separately as equivalent all-age populations which have some degree of exchange.

Table 2 Status of the grey seal in Great Britain in 1985 (NERC, 1987)

About 24,000 grey seal pups are probably born annually on the coasts of Great Britain, with perhaps another thousand in Ireland (Hewer, 1974), of which 12,600 (about half) are born in the Hebrides (including North Rona). From knowledge of the population age structure, the total number of seals can be estimated from the number of pups born. This shows that about 53% of grey seals in Britain live in the Hebrides making up one-third of the world population.

A glance at the map (Fig. 3) shows that isolation and lack of disturbance by man has a strong bearing upon the distribution of the grey seal in its choice of breeding sites. Almost without exception in the Hebrides, the colonies are on small seldom-visited islands, though these may be within sight of an inhabited shore across a narrow sound as at Nave Island (Islay), Eilein Ghaoideamul (Oronsay) and Gunna (Tiree). The breeding distribution is shown in Table 3. In recent years, the grey seal population has increased at 3–7% per annum in the Hebrides, depending on the colony. However, a recent epidemic of a distemper-like disease amongst seals in Europe may have temporarily reduced this rate of increase.

Island	1961	1968	1976	1981
Outer Hebrides				
Monach Isles	50	200	2575	
North Rona	2600	2200*	2500	
Gasker	1094	1400	2340	
Shillay	150	200	690	
Coppay	80	150	515	
Haskeir	113	—	385	
Causamul	84	200	270	
Deasker	17	—	75	
Outer Hebrides	4200	4350	9350	
Inner Hebrides				
Treshnish Isles				755
Oronsay+				745
Gunna				235
Nave Is. Islay				105
Others #				100
Inner Hebrides				1940

* Boyd and Campbell, 1971
+ Eilein nan Ron and Eilein Ghaoideamal (Oronsay)
# Jura (40), Rum (30) and a few on each of Canna, Coll, Tiree and Skye.

Table 3 Estimates of production of grey seal pups in the Outer Hebrides in 1978 (Boyd, 1963; Bonner, 1976; Summers, 1978) and the Inner Hebrides in 1981 (Vaughan, 1983).

When we began our work on grey seals in the Hebrides we inherited from Fraser Darling the concept that the stocks on the various breeding islands were biologically (genetically)

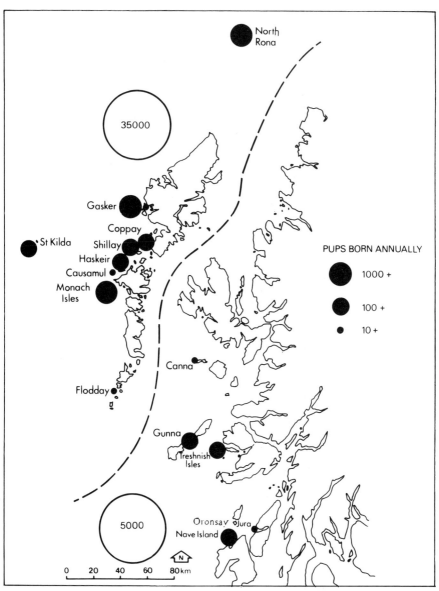

Fig. 3
*Distribution of grey
seal breeding grounds
in the Hebrides (after
Summers and
Harwood, 1979 and
Vaughan, 1983)*

separate; he drew attention to differences in the coat colour of
the stocks that he studied at the Treshnish Isles and North
Rona. The programme of work that started for the Nature
Conservancy at North Rona in the late fifties, and which has
been continued by us and others ever since, has shown that
there is probably little, if any, such separation and that, while

the choice of breeding grounds seems to be mainly confined to the long-established sites listed in Table 3, there is interchange between them. Young bulls and cows branded on North Rona have subsequently been found breeding on the Monach Isles, and from this it has been estimated that at least 8% of the seals on the Monach Isles are of North Rona stock (Harwood, Anderson and Curry, 1976).

Further evidence of recruitment to breeding islands of 'outside' offspring is found in the rate of increase in the size of the assembly on the Monach Isles. In the period 1961–76, the number of pups born there increased steadily from 50 to 2575 per annum, which would have been impossible without recruitment from other islands. However, some degree of separation probably exists between stocks in different sectors of the British coast. For instance, the timing of the breeding season differs in different sectors; the first pups to be born each year are on the coast of South Wales in September while the last are born at Scroby Sands, Norfolk, in December. The spread of births in the Hebrides, including North Rona, is from the beginning of October to mid-November. However, there is an earlier start by about a week in the more southerly assemblies on the Treshnish Isles and Oronsay, where the peak of pupping occurs about 2nd October, than on North Uist and Harris, where the peak is about 7th, and on North Rona, where the peak is later still, occurring about 10th October.

The Breeding Cycle of the Grey Seal

The breeding cycle of the grey seal which, before Fraser Darling's time fifty years ago was a mystery, is now well known. During the spring and summer, the nursery islands hold few seals and the breeding grounds above high watermark have none at all. Where the seals from all the breeding islands go at this time is largely unknown. However, judging by reports of marked young seals from North Rona, the dispersal may be over 650km from the breeding site; sightings range from Donegal (530km), to south-east Iceland (750km) and south-west Norway (720km). However, the young seals may not necessarily follow their seniors to these distant shores; they may wander far from the 'normal' range or be carried far by sea currents. The population probably scatters from all the breeding islands to favourite feeding grounds where they can quickly make good their loss of condition through breeding, though most of them probably remain within 150km, since although they leave the breeding islands *en masse* in October and November, many return there to moult in January and

February. Both bulls and cows occur in these moulting assemblies, but the late winter is a particularly important time for the cows; the fertilised ovum forms a blastocyst and remains dormant in the uterus for about 3 months after mating, becoming implanted in the wall of the uterus. Seals, together with other sundry species such as the roe deer and the eastern spotted skunk, are unusual in having delayed implantation, the end of which roughly coincides with the time of moult. In a few weeks, the seals will have changed their coats and be off again to their hunting, the females with their growing embryos.

During the summer dispersal, seals from different breeding islands must come to share the same feeding grounds. The bulls are first to begin the return to the breeding grounds, gathering from late July onwards on rocks which, earlier in the year, were occupied by the moulting assemblies.

By late August, the bulls have been joined by cows on the rocks adjacent to the breeding grounds; they are heavily pregnant, and usually closer to the water than the bulls. They also sleep less soundly, and will be the first to slip into the water at the slightest sign of danger. There is much fidgeting and calling in soft, haunting voices. At North Rona the resting rocks are on Gealldruig Mhor and Loba Sgeir, which are the thresholds of the nursery grounds on Fianuis and Sceapull.

The build up in the numbers of bulls and cows occurs synchronously. Breeding bulls will normally weigh between 250 and 300kg and are over 2m long. Only the prime bulls will be successful at retaining a position on the breeding grounds, where competition for a place can be fierce. Few bulls under the age of 10 will win through and, even when old enough,

Grey seal bull's head showing the wide dark eyes and the vibrissae on the muzzle and forehead said to detect movements of prey in the sea (Photo J. M. Boyd)

sheer physical size is important. Bulls must also bring ashore significant body reserves, because the most successful will stay for up to 8 weeks without leaving to feed or drink. This is a significant drain on their resources and few will probably manage to defend a position on the breeding grounds for more than 3 or 4 years running. Throughout the breeding period the aim of a grey seal bull is to station himself in those areas of a colony where females are most likely to give birth, feed their pups and come into oestrus.

At North Rona, the gullies on Fianuis are a narrow main access for a heavy traffic of lumbering adults. The seals here are more densely packed, and in a constant state of agitation with much fighting of bulls and bickering and snapping of cows. By the middle of October this is a foul ghetto of the seals' own making—a muddy quagmire and a string of septic pools dotted with the pathetic bodies of bloated pups. Even more pathetic are the starving orphans with puss-filled eyes, contrasting with the fat, fluffy youngsters on the wide space of the hinterland where the turf remains intact and conditions are better.

From the Fank (sheep fold) Brae above the promontory of Fianuis it is possible to watch the seals closely, out of range of scent and sight. Among the many bobbing heads around the east landing on the sheltered side, there is one looking intently inland, often stretching to see the other seals already ashore. The dappled silvery throat and short nose shows it to be a cow, possibly about to deliver her first pup. In a few moments she is ashore and desperately hauling herself clear of the surf breaking upon her back and splaying upon the slabs in front of her. Her wet, blue-grey back shines like polished steel. An embattled bull—dull by comparison—hurrying to escape an adversary, inspects her as she makes her way up the slabs. A quick snap and lunge sees him off to the sea. It is now obvious that she is pregnant, and she is clean and fresh compared with the other seals which have been ashore for a week or more. Her bulk is due less to her unborn pup than to the thick layer of blubber fat she is carrying to see herself and her pup through the 18 days of lactation.

At the top of the shore rocks she sees the other seals already distributed over the swards ahead. She is cautious, moving one lurch at a time, looking anxiously around her and sniffing the air. A fracas close-by frightens her and she quickly turns towards the sea, but, reassured, resumes her progress inland. Finding her way barred by other cows warding her off as she approaches their pups, she is compelled to zig-zag through the colony in a series of minor conflicts until, eventually, she reaches 'clear' ground at the old bothy by the storm beach, which flanks the cliff-top on the west side. She has traversed the peninsula and has reached the far fringe, almost on the western, cliff-bound coast. However, she has found her pupping spot and lies quiet awaiting her time of delivery. This journey from the sea, though arduous, is not a record; a few bulls and cows breed on the ridge at the top of the Fank Brae from where we are observing, about 40m above and 450m from the sea.

Births are rarely seen; that is mainly because of the visual disadvantage of most observers in viewing the herd from the flat, but also because of the rapid delivery of the foetus in a few minutes, sometimes even in seconds. the first indication of a birth at North Rona is a noisy scuffle of gulls over the afterbirth during which a bird is sometimes maimed by the reactive cow. A few hapless great black-backed gulls stalk the colony dragging broken wings.

After an hour our attention returns to the cow by the bothy and we find a thin yellowish pup lying beside her; she has succeeded in warding-off the gulls which, having devoured the afterbirth, linger on the ruined bothy, still hopeful of having the pup as well. The pup is helpless, though it instinctively nuzzles at the mother searching for a nipple. The touch of the infant on her flank makes her keel over on one side to expose her belly and pivot round to present her nipples to the pup. She may also appear to guide the little one towards her nipples by waving her flipper. The two nipples, normally inverted in the streamlining of her body for swimming, are then everted and the pup attaches and sucks in the first hour of its life. Feeding occurs about five times in 24 hours at regular intervals. The seal cow's milk has a fat content of 50% compared with the 3.5% of the dairy cow, and the pup probably drinks this rich milk as fast as it is produced by the mother; it weighs about 14kg at birth and 40kg when weaned about 17 days later—putting on over 1.5kg per day! This increase in weight is achieved by little growth in length from 82cm at birth to 90cm at weaning; most of the weight increase is caused by a thickening layer of blubber under the skin. Needless to say, the cow loses weight by about 4kg per day and at time of weaning, she is barely two-thirds of her weight on coming ashore, about 170kg. In contrast to her plump condition on arrival in the colony, she departs lean, almost skinny, but not before she has been mated by one or more of the bulls.

From our observation post on Fank Brae it is possible to pick out the bulls from the cows; they are fewer (1 in 10 in the dense colony) larger, and generally darker in colour. They are well spaced through the colony and do not lie closely packed as they would on the offshore rocks. On the fringes of the colony, and in the sea immediately offshore, there are many other bulls ready to move in and take the place of tired bulls. Bulls, unlike cows, continue to grow in size through life and the older, bigger bulls probably occupy the breeding grounds early in the season.

Bulls first come into breeding condition when they are 5 or 6 years old, and most of them are dead by the time they are 15; a few live longer but rarely over 20 years old. Cows also attain puberty when five or six years old, but live longer than bulls; most are dead by the time they are 20, but a few live longer occasionally to over 30 years and sometimes, though rarely, over 40.

There is an air of reluctant toleration of each other among the resident bulls. Each keeps its distance but does not miss an opportunity of extending its chances of mating and of challenging the advance of neighbouring bulls or intruders. These encounters follow a pattern: the lumbering intruder halts when he sees the territory holder advancing; lowering his head flat along the ground and opening his mouth showing his teeth, he hisses; the challenger may do likewise, the two may then advance, and an energetic clash can follow with contestants snarling and gripping each other by the folds of skin on the neck, flipper and tail. The fight is usually short-lived but, despite the toughness of the skin in these animals, some deep wounds can be inflicted. Fights to the death probably never happen. Usually, however, the challenge does not come to blows and the challenger makes off back to the sea or to a safe distance.

An intruding challenger which has come to the rear of the colony by a fringe route passing further and further from the sea can find himself in deep trouble. In the heat of the moment he has turned into the colony, to find himself surrounded by resident bulls, and he chooses the shortest route to the sea. This is a savage gauntlet of running fights with perhaps six or more big bulls, ending with a headlong plunge into the sea. We have seen a bull which had fallen to its death over a cliff, probably as a result of such a chase.

Copulation commences with the cow coming on 'heat' towards the end of the nursing period, some 15–18 days after giving birth. A day or two may pass before she will allow the bull to mate. He will grasp her by the neck but only to facilitate his successful mounting, and afterwards they will lie quietly for up to 15 minutes. Mating also takes place in the sea. In the deep channels at Eilein nan Ron, Oronsay, there is evidence of bulls holding 'territory' in sheltered waters opposite small pupping beaches. During coition, the pair are submerged, only surfacing to breathe.

During the 18-day nursing period the pup has grown rapidly, and partially moulted its thick birth coat. By the end of the first month of life it has little or no white fur and is clad instead in its short, sea-going coat. The female pups have blue-grey heads and backs with light underparts, often with faint grey flecks. The males are dark grey, sometimes jet black, with faint grey flecking on flanks and belly. Wide-eyed, they face the world with pulsing nostrils, trembling vibrissae and tiny glistening teeth set in a delicate pink mouth; the milk teeth are shed *in utero*. Without warning, they are deserted by their mothers, and at little more than a fortnight old, they have to fend for themselves.

Grey seal cow and recently born pup on North Rona. The pup's white coat is cast during the nursing period and before it puts to sea (Photo J. M. Boyd)

Pup mortality is high. If the little ones survive the ravages of the gulls, the bites of jealous, quarrelsome cows, infection and the crushings by both bulls and cows, they face the hazards of sea-going without the guidance and protection of parents. Well equipped as they are with a sleek, waterproof and heatproof coat and layer of blubber, provisioned with nourishment to see them through the learning-to-feed period, and having the instincts to avoid danger and defend themselves against an enemy (try handling one!), many perish in their first year. About half of the pups born never live to see their first birthday.

Mortality of pups is much lower on colonies like the Monach Isles, Shillay (Harris) and the Treshnish Isles (<12%) — where the seals pup on clean sand or wave- and rain-washed rocky platforms—than on North Rona or Gasker (>20%) where the turf soon breaks and where infection may be harboured in the soil.

Conservation and Management of the Grey Seal

The increase in numbers of grey seals, which can be traced back to the last century, still continues. The fishing industry claims that seals cause significant damage to fisheries through predation on catchable stocks of fish, codworm parasites and damage to fishing gear. The situation is made more serious by the decline in available fish stocks in areas frequented by seals, but for reasons other than seal predation; the continuous exploitation of fish stocks by man over the last century, with ever greater efficiency in fishing technology. Parrish and Shearer (1977) estimated that 65,000 tonnes of fish ($£$15–20 million at 1974 prices), were 'lost to seals' annually in the UK. About 85% is attributed to grey seals (55,000 tonnes), of which about 28,000 tonnes may be taken in the Hebrides. However, these estimates were obtained using highly dubious measurements of the grey seal diet and food requirements. In 1981, the Sea Mammal Research Unit (NERC) produced a more realistic estimate of fish consumption by grey seals. It seems that 60% of the diet may be sand-eels, while cod, whiting, saithe, pollack, haddock, ling and many other species make up the remaining 40%. They estimated that, on average, a grey seal will eat about 5 kg of fish each day, which means that the British grey seals eat 84,000–215,000 tonnes of fish each year. It would, of course, be unrealistic to translate this figure into an estimate of financial loss to the fishing industry because the great majority of fish eaten by grey seals probably have no commercial value.

The case put against the seals by certain fishermen and fish farmers whose stations are continuously visited by persistently roguish seals is irrefutable, and the fishermen are legally entitled to defend their stations in a humane way by shooting the intruders with a rifle. However, this raises another problem, because there are now many fish farms in the sea lochs of the Hebrides and all these will defend their nets against seals. Killing is neither regulated nor monitored, so this could be a major new source of mortality for seals that could affect their populations.

In 1977, NERC advised on how to stabilise grey-seal stocks in Britain at the mid-1960's level, and how to maintain a sustainable pup harvest with maximum gain in scientific information. Since the grey seal is polygamous, little or no control of numbers can be achieved by culling bulls; measures of control can only be applied by culling pups and adult cows or a combination of both. Such operations on the breeding grounds causes disturbance, the escape of many cows to sea and the desertion and orphaning of suckling pups. Highly organised operations in ideal weather may achieve the desired objective, but operations are often disrupted by storms resulting with difficulties in seamanship, shooting, taking samples from the dead seals, recording and disposal of carcasses. Considering the Outer Hebrides and Orkney as a single stock, the NERC scientists stated that the population could be reduced to the desired mid-1960s level by either culling 6000 pups and 6000 cows in one year with a pup cull of 6000 thereafter, or in a sliding scale of annual culls up to a ten-year period with 4000 pups and 700 cows annually with 4000 pups annually thereafter. The effects of such culls on the population, however, are unpredictable since there is no way of making a consistent choice of animals to be killed; while older cows may hold their ground and be shot, younger cows may put to sea at the sound of the first shot and not return during the culling operation.

The shooting of hundreds of cows and pups annually in the National Nature Reserves of North Rona and Monach Isles which, together with the small seal islands off Harris, Treshnish Isles and Oronsay are Sites of Special Scientific Interest under the Wildlife and Countryside Act, should require quite irrefutable scientific justification. So far, despite strenuous efforts by fishery biologists, a directly significant connection between grey seals and the general status of available commercial fisheries has not been proven (except locally—often by common seals). The suggested cull to a level of the mid-1960s will logically reduce the number of fish taken by grey seals, but is unlikely to cause any significant rise in the general income of fishermen.

Common Seal

The distinction between grey and common seals has rarely been made in the literature of the Hebrides, though Martin (1703), referring to the Outer Hebrides, states:

those (seals) on the east side, who are of lesser stature (than the grey seal), bring forth their young in the midle of June

This is a clear identification of the common seal. Today, they still frequent the sheltered eastern coasts and sounds of the Outer Hebrides, and also are widespread in the Inner Hebrides (Vaughan, 1983). They are very confiding, and provide an exciting spectacle for sightseers on ferries, yachts and tripper-boats around Gigha, in the Firth of Lorne, Loch Linnhe and the Sounds of Mull, Iona and Sleat. Ferry passengers are likely to see common seals in summer in the rockbound approaches to Port Ellen, Islay; Arinagour, Coll; Canna Harbour; Castlebay, Barra; Lochboisdale; Lochmaddy; Tarbert, Harris; Stornoway and in crossings of the Sounds of Barra, Eriskay and Harris, Kyle of Lochalsh and Kylerhea where the Forestry Commission have built a hide to observe seals and otters. The common seal is mainly of dark brown appearance, but due to a varying intensity of light speckling can vary in colour from almost uniform dark brown to light fawn or, more rarely, creamy white.

The bulls are somewhat larger than the cows, but this is not as obvious as in the grey seal; adult bulls are 1.5 to 2m long and cows, 1.3 to 1.5m. They weigh about 100kg. The breeding biology is still unclear; scientists cannot examine this species as they do the grey seal, since pupping and mating does not take place in quick succession while ashore. Common seal pups are born on tidal strands in the Hebrides between mid-June and mid-July; at birth they are about 85cm in length and weigh about 9kg. Suckling lasts from four to six weeks, bringing the pup's weight to about 26kg at weaning, and the cow comes into oestrus at the end of lactation. The moult probably takes place in August. Like the grey seal, common seals have a delayed implantation of the fertilised ovum (blastocyst) of about 12 weeks, and a gestation period of 8 months.

Though the haul-outs of common seals are reasonably well known, little is known about the numerical status of the species; unlike the grey seal it has not been possible to count the common seal pups and to calculate from that the total population. However, they are so widely distributed and generally present in small numbers, particularly on sheltered coasts, the Hebrides must hold many thousands. Common seals in the Hebrides remained largely unaffected by the epidemic of a distemper-like disease in 1988. In company with grey seals they have been hunted since prehistoric times and bones have been recorded from archeological sites (Clarke, 1946). Before the Conservation of Seals Act (1970), there was no protection for the common seal in Britain, but in historical times it is unlikely that many were taken before the use of the rifle. In the decade 1971–81, an average of 240 common seal pups were killed annually in the Hebrides under a commercial licence, in addition to others of all ages that have been legitimately shot by fishermen and fish farmers protecting their nets and cages.

The movements of common seals probably depend much on

local conditions. While many probably feed along the sheltered shores of sea lochs, they will also move many miles out to sea to feed. Observations of common seals in Orkney showed this to be the case—individuals will make foraging trips to sea of several days duration, and we have observed large seasonal fluctuations in numbers of common seals at sites in the Hebrides. While observers at Davaar Island (Campbelltown), Ronachan (Kintyre), Isle Oronsay (Skye) reported large numbers of common seals in spring and summer, those at West Kilbride and Head of Ayr (Ayrshire), Carradale (Kintyre), Lough Foyle, McArthur's Head (Islay) and Lady's Rock (Lismore) reported large numbers in autumn and winter. Some of these changes may be local redistributions, but more distant seasonal movements cannot be ruled out. The numbers present at a site will also change according to the state of moult of the population, and these factors have to be included in any estimate of population size derived from one-off counts of seals at haul-out sites.

At some sites, common seals patrol the sheltered coasts, sea-lochs and inner sounds, usually singly. They tend to feed at high tide; the rest of the time is spent sleeping on the leeward side of rocks, safe from disturbance but conveniently close to their radius of hunting. Occasionally they are joined by grey seals and while juvenile greys may mix with the commons, the adults usually remain apart on other skerries. Many such situations are in the path of migratory sea-trout and salmon, and within easy reach of salmon-fishing stations and fish farms. There is little wonder, therefore, that the common seal has a particularly bad reputation and is shot on sight when it ventures near such installations.

The seals of the Hebrides have given both of us that sense of wonderment in nature without which there is no driving force in biology, and provided us with a rousing professional challenge. We were initially inspired by the work of our late mentor and friend Sir Frank Fraser Darling on North Rona and Treshnish before the last war (Boyd, 1986), and in the fifties and sixties the late Professor H.R. Hewer, whose book *British Seals* (1974) in this series is the standard work on the subject. In the seventies and eighties we worked with W.N. Bonner, C.F. Summers, Sheila Anderson, Mike Fedak and the late R.W. (Bill) Vaughan, who tragically lost his life while studying seals in the Wash. The sense of companionship which attended the work, which was focused to a great extent on North Rona, the Monach Isles and the Harris islands, still lives on. However, despite our best efforts, the seals still hold many of their secrets close to themselves.

CHAPTER 4

The Wildfowl Islands

Islay

Many things combine to make the Hebrides a very special place for the naturalist: the flowers of the machair islands; the seabirds of St Kilda; the red deer of Rum; the grey seals of North Rona—the geese of Islay. Indeed, Islay is the wildfowl island *par excellence*, with a great extent and variety of coastal and wetland habitats. There is an agricultural tradition in Islay possibly dating back to Bronze Age times, and this saw great expansion in the Middle Ages to the population maximum in the early 19th century, since when farming has replaced crofting-type landuse. Today, Islay resembles the Highland-Lowland fringe of the Scottish mainland, with good-sized tenant farms on estates of declining size and prosperity. In the last century, the estates have been managed as sporting land *inter alia* for wildfowl, with protection of the wildfowl grounds for private shooting. The main overwintering stocks consist of: up to 22,000 barnacle geese (*Branta leucopsis*), 7,000 Greenland white-fronted geese (*Anser albiforns flavirostris*), 3,000 eider (*Somateria mollissima*), 1,500 scaup (*Aythya marila*), 800 teal (*Anas crecca*), 500 wigeon (*Anas penelope*), 100–500 each of mallard (*Anas platyrhynchos*), shelduck (*Tadorna tadorna*), less than 100 greylag geese (*Anser anser*) and pochard (*Aythya ferina*). Since the wildfowl grounds of Islay are of national and international importance (many of the wintering species breed in other countries), the NCC has notified them as SSSI's (Figs. 5 & 6) and has devised a scheme for compensating farmers for the grazing of geese within the SSSI's; also the RSPB runs the farm of Aoradh at Gruinart as a wildfowl reserve in the heart of the barnacle goose ground (the geese of Islay became a *cause célèbre* in nature conservation in the mid-1980s).

Barnacle Goose

From mid-October to mid-April, barnacle geese that nest in East Greenland occupy north-west Scotland and Ireland.

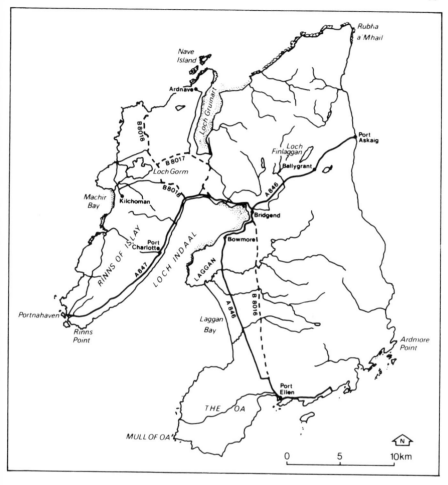

Fig. 4
Location map of Islay

These form a population of about 30,000 birds, distinct from those that nest in Spitzbergen, which spend the winter on the Solway. The main body occupies the Hebrides, with small well-separated flocks on south Orkney and the mainland seaboards of Sutherland, Wester Ross and Argyll. The headquarters of the species is in Islay, and at the peaks of numbers in November and March the island may hold over 27,500, almost 90% of the Greenland stock (Table 13.1), which for a short time in autumn, assembles in Islay before dispersing to Ireland and other wintering grounds in the Hebrides (Easterbee *et al.*, 1987). Clearly, Gruinart, which in autumn may hold *c.* 74% of the stock, is a focal point in the annual migration of the Greenland barnacle geese, and is a very important area in their conservation (p. 245).

Island Group	March 1973	March/April 1978	March/April 1983	March 1988
Islay	15,000	21,000	14,000	20,200
Treshnish Isles	420	610	620	378
Tiree/Coll	145	390	620	550
Barra Sound	335	455	375	431
Isay (Skye)	295	290	250	245
Monach Isles	640	760	640	715
Harris Sound	980	1,330	1,555	1,007
Shiant Isles	450	420	420	532
Scotland	19,740	28,060	20,820	26,957
Ireland	4,400	5,760	4,430	7,594
Total	24,140	33,820	25,250	34,551

Table 4 Number of Greenland barnacle geese counted in aerial surveys of their main haunts (Ogilvie 1983a and *in litt.* 1988—the figures are rounded by Thom, 1986 and are not peak counts).

The barnacle geese in Islay are distributed throughout the pasturelands, which have been improved by agriculture over the centuries, and which have been used in recent decades in modern grass-intensive husbandry, supporting herds of dairy and beef cattle. However, a decline in dairy husbandry in the 1980s has probably affected the distribution of the geese. Concentrations are centred on Gruinart, Bridgend and Laggan, between which there is probably much exchange. A large number of birds that roost at Gruinart use the Loch Gorm area for feeding (Figs. 4 & 5).

The population has been counted annually in November, after the main influx of birds has arrived from Greenland, and in March/April before the main exodus departs to their Arctic breeding grounds. In the 1960s and 70s, counts in January showed a slightly smaller population in mid-winter, possibly caused by winter mortality through shooting and natural causes, followed by some immigration into Islay from elsewhere. After the shooting season in February and March, the pastures of the Hebrides are at the lowest point of annual productivity, and at this time, the improved fields of Islay are clearly more attractive to between 2,000 and 3,000 geese than the threadbare, withered machairs and sheep-walks of neighbouring islands and the mainland coast. Before making the long flight to Greenland and entering upon the rigours of the breeding season, the geese require a build-up of body condi-

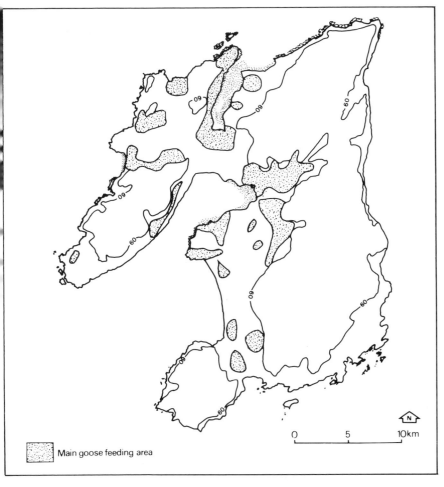

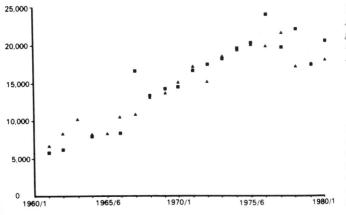

Fig. 5
Map showing the main
goose wintering grounds
in Islay (from Ogilvie,
1983)

Fig. 6
Graph showing the
increase in numbers of
barnacle geese
wintering in Islay
between 1960 and 1980
(from Ogilvie, 1983)

tion which, in the southern Hebrides, can best be achieved in the reseeded and fertilised cattle pastures of Islay.

Between 1961 and 1981 the number of barnacle geese wintering in Islay increased from about 6,000 to 20,000 (Ogilvie, 1983b). The data are plotted in Fig. 6, and five key counts of the 20 given by Ogilvie are shown in Table 5, which also gives data on recruitment, total Greenland population, and the percentage of that total wintering in Islay.

Winter	Nov	Mar/Apr	Change	% young	Greenland	% Islay
1961–2	5,800	6,800	+1,000	10.7	14,000	41.4
1965–6	nc	8,300	—	11.2	20,000	45.0
1972–3	17,300	15,000	−2,300	12.1	24,000	71.2
1977–8	19,600	21,000	+1,900	4.9	33,000	65.2
nc = no count						

Table 5   Four key counts of barnacle geese in Islay in November and March/April 1961-81, showing numbers on Islay, percentages of young in Islay, percentages of the total Greenland population in Islay, and data on changes in numbers (after Ogilvie 1983b).

The annual population on Islay is the total number of survivors of the previous year, including first-year young. Mortality is measured by subtracting the current autumn total, *excluding* first-year birds, from the autumn total of the previous year, *including* first-year birds. Over twenty years the average annual mortality was 9.6% which corresponds with 10% for the Spitzbergen population on the Solway. Though there was some immigration to Islay in the course of each winter, there has been no significant regional redistribution of stocks throughout this twenty-year period. Recruitment, therefore, is measured by the percentage of first-year birds present in the flocks, and has averaged 14%. The higher value of recruitment over mortality is consistent with a population which has increased by a factor of three in 20 years. In the early 1980s, recruitment declined mainly because of poor breeding success and increased shooting. This resulted in a decline in the population, but reduced shooting in recent years has caused numbers to return to the high levels of the 1970s.

Bag-records in the 1960s and early 1970s, show 500–700 barnacle geese shot by estates in winter, and to that total must be added those shot by farmers and others. However, as the population increased in the 1970s, farmers became more and more strident in their complaints of damage done to their grazings by huge flocks of geese, so the shooting season for geese (1st September to 31st January) was extended until 20th February below high-water mark. There was also an increase in

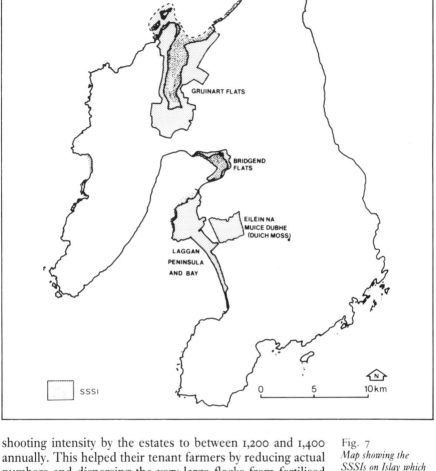

GRUINART FLATS

BRIDGEND
FLATS

EILEIN NA
MUICE DUBHE
(DUICH MOSS)

LAGGAN
PENINSULA
AND BAY

SSSI

0   5   10km

shooting intensity by the estates to between 1,200 and 1,400
annually. This helped their tenant farmers by reducing actual
numbers and dispersing the very large flocks from fertilised
and reseeded fields. The estates also let the shooting to a few
hotels, and there was extra income to be had from shooting by
visitors. In the mid-1980s, the NCC notified the main goose
grounds of Islay as three SSSIs, including part of the new
RSPB Reserve at Aoradh (Fig. 7), and there followed a
scheme to compensate farmers for the grazing of geese on their
land situated within the SSSIs at Gruinart, Laggan and
Bridgend. Outside the SSSIs, farmers obtain licences to shoot,
or otherwise move, barnacle geese from their land, hopefully
into the SSSIs. While this arrangement does not give full protection to the barnacle goose, the species is unmolested in its

Fig. 7
*Map showing the
SSSIs on Islay which
are of special interest
because of wintering
wildfowl, particularly
barnacle and white-
fronted geese which
breed in Greenland
(Updated from Kerr
and Boyd, 1983)*

Barnacle geese in flight in Islay (Photo Morley Hedley)

favourite grounds. Unfortunately however, the scheme is not satisfactory to all farmers, especially those whose improved fields are close to the boundaries of the SSSIs, but outside them, and do not qualify for compensation.

Greenland White-fronted Goose

The world population of the white-fronted goose (*Anser albifrons flavirostris*) breeding in West Greenland and wintering in Britain, now amounts to about 21,000 birds. During the autumns of 1982–84, the numbers in Britain increased under protection—1982: 7,200; 1983: 8,200; 1984, 9,490; 1985; 11,026; 1986; 10,809. Islay held 45–56% of the British stock (20–25% of the world stock) in November 1986 with a wide scatter of smaller concentrations notably in Tiree/Coll, Kintyre and Galloway (Table 13.3).

Island Group	Nov 1982	Nov 1983	Nov 1984	Mar/Apr 1985
O. Hebrides	89	99	114	15
Skye/Sm. Is	96	98	106	108
Tiree	372	357	620	750
Coll	343	435	441	179
Islay	3, 250	4,592	5,256	4,715
Other Areas				
NE Scot'd	457	315	376	518
N. Argyll*	158	193	243	181
S. Argyll	1,723	1,342	1,659	1,635
Galloway	595	683	633	713
England	33	1	10	13
Wales	73	93	76	88
Totals	7,189	8,188	9,490	8,997

*Data do not include those of Tiree/Coll nor of Islay all of which are given separately; they include data from Kintyre where 1,276 and 940 were counted in November 1982 and 1983 respectively; they also include 118 and 134 respectively from Loch Lomond.

Table 6 The distribution of Greenland white-fronted geese in the Hebrides in 1982–85 compiled from Thom 1986 and Stroud (1984).

The increase in numbers in Scotland from 4,000–5,000 in the 1950s to 7,000–8,000 in the 1980s has been accompanied by a decline in Ireland from about 15,000 to 8,000–9,000, of which 5,000–6,000 are on the Wexford Slobs, (Ogilvie 1983b). This decline is attributed mainly to the draining of bogs, widespread disturbance, and shooting. In Islay, the white-fronts are scattered widely over the island, frequenting a different range to the barnacles, but overlapping with them. While the great barnacle goose flocks roost far out on the tidal flats and on secure land such as Nave Island, the white-fronted spend the night mainly on lochs and bogs. During the day they move in small flocks composed of family groups of up to a few hundred individuals. They feed on stubbles and rush-meadows, and are sometimes seen among the barnacle geese on improved pastures.

In the period 1966–82 the white-fronted goose population fluctuated between 2,500 and 4,000, with percentages of first-year birds ranging from 4.6 to 26.1 (Ogilvie, 1983b). The average rate of recruitment from 1962–86 was 14.8% per annum, while the average rate of loss was 10.5% per annum. How many of these recruits might be immigrants from Ireland

Locality	1981/82	1982/83	1983/84	1984/85	1985/86	1986/87
Oa	540	758	865	1,232	1,286	1,128
Ardtulla	0	0	0	95	0	27
Gruinart	322	114	415	884	633	70
Gorm	232	197	454	390	349	675
Rhinns	396	657	504	217	802	1,641
Laggan	527	444	646	777	1,005	740
Glen	475	174	350	340	60	345
Kilmeny	1,096	1,535	1,358	1,321	2,197	1,860
Totals	3,588	3,879	4,592	5,256	6,332	6,486

Table 7 Autumn distribution of white-fronted geese in Islay in the eighties (Stroud 1984, 1985 unpublished).

is unknown. Today, the white-fronted goose is completely protected in Scotland, but since licences can be obtained for shooting other species of geese, and the white-fronts often live close to barnacles and greylags, many are probably accidentally shot. Illegal shooting of white-fronts in the small, widely scattered flocks throughout the Hebrides still continues.

A large flock of barnacle geese taking off at Gruinart Flats which lie within an SSSI and partly within an RSPB Reserve (Photo Morley Hedley)

The danger to this race of geese by the reclamation of moorland for forestry, and the extraction of peat for industrial purposes, posed a threat to the future of stocks in Islay, as it has done over many years in Ireland. In 1985–86, development and conservation interests were brought into conflict in Islay over

the proposals to extract peat for distilling from Eilean na Muice Dubh (Duich Moss), a main roost of white-fronted geese. Another proposal to afforest moorland on the Rhinns, used by white-fronts, was also in contention. These issues of white-fronted goose conservation on Islay assumed national and international importance, because Duich Moss and much of the Rhinns are SSSI's, and the white-fronted goose is a species protected under the Wildlife and Countryside Act and European Council of Minister's Directive on the Conservation of Wild Birds. These two factors effectively brought the conservation of the white-fronts and their wintering areas in Islay within the sphere of British domestic law, and in 1987 political pressures resulted in the distillers seeking and obtaining sufficient peat for their purposes in another less prestigious bog on the island.

Greylag Goose

With the thousands of wintering Greenland barnacle and white-fronted geese on Islay, there are a few hundred greylag geese (*Anser anser*), which arrive in early October and depart in early April. There is no recent breeding record of greylag in Islay, the breeding stronghold in the Hebrides being in the Uists and Benbecula. Boyd and Ogilvie (1972) thought that the greylags in Islay belonged to the indigenous native stock from north-west Scotland and were not Icelandic birds; this was based on the similar observed percentages of young birds in stocks from Islay and north-west Scotland. Greylags have never been numerous in Islay (Booth, 1981) and have been in steady decline since the 1950s when 500–600 birds frequented the fields and saltings around Islay House—now there are less than 100 in the same localities.

Tiree, Gunna and Coll

Goose-watching was a common activity of ours on a winter's day in Tiree. Starting on the Reef, we walked along the east bank of An Fhaodhail. On the left there were two square kilometres of rush meadow and fields of improved pasture and stubble; on the right rocky heath, fringed with small green fields of cattle-grazed pasture. Our quest for geese in such habitat was short-lived for, as we came in sight of the ruins of Odhrasgair, we put up a flock of about 40 Greenland white-fronts calling wildly to all their kith-and-kin across the flats towards Balephetrish and Kenovay. The ponds and watercourses held whooper and mute swans, teal, mallard, pochard, tufted duck and goldeneye, and the noise of the white-fronts sent a wave of unrest throughout the populace.

By the time we had reached the road at Balephetrish, we had counted over 300 of them—most of the stock wintering in Tiree (Table 6), and there were about 30 greylags in small groups among the white-fronts. However, there was no sign of barnacle geese until we had climbed Balephetrish Hill. Turning our backs upon the spacious rushy flats in the centre of the island, we were now in a different habitat—a ragged ribbon of green grass between sea and moor, running away as far as the eye could see to Coll. There, about 500m away, in their typical Hebridean setting of sea-meadows above the Atlantic breakers, grazed a tight pack of about 150 barnacle geese.

We were standing at the southern limit of the barnacle goose range in Tiree, Gunna and Coll. If we were to walk northwards we would drive them all before us and obtain little idea of the size of the population. Therefore we decided to drive to Miodar on the Gunna Sound and walk southward by the shores of Salum and Vaul. The barnacles which forage on Tiree flighted in the afternoon to roost on Gunna and we had them flying towards us. Hidden in the rocky country, there was great excitement as the flocks came flying low overhead, rearing upwards as we suddenly came into their view.

In recent winters, 400–600 barnacle geese have roosted on the Gunna roost. Some move northward to Ballyhaugh on Coll and others to the north coast of Tiree as far south as Saltaig to feed. The 300–400 white-fronted geese occupy the wetlands, stubble and improved pastures across the waist of Tiree from Balephetrish Bay to Hynish Bay, and about 100 greylag geese occupy a wide area of western Tiree between Loch Bhasapol and Loch a'Phuil and eastward to Kenovay—a few pairs of greylags have bred in Coll since the 1930s (Boyd, 1958) and are increasing, with a report of breeding in Tiree in 1986. White-fronts are fully protected and barnacles are also protected but can be shot under licence by farmers and crofters to protect crops. There are no sporting licences for these species, but greylags may be shot between 1st September and 31st January, which provides a loophole for the unscrupulous shooter. For example, two tame Canada geese (*Branta canadensis*), possibly visiting from Colonsay, which we observed in April 1986 in Tiree, were shot on the ground in the following winter by a foreign visitor. This species, like greylags, may be shot without licence, but such an incident is indicative of the low prevailing level of sportsmanship to which the protected species are exposed in remote places by some shooting parties.

The Uists and Benbecula

From the late 1950s to the late 1960s, those of us in the Nature Conservancy who had the job of setting up and managing the Loch Druidibeg National Nature Reserve in South Uist, had the memorable experience of staying with Mrs Annie Flora MacDonald on the shores of the loch. Having been the wife of a famous gamekeeper, possessing the 'second sight', and having been in service at Balmoral, 'herself' was a person of outstanding Gaelic character. We breakfasted at her kitchen window, where we could see the native greylag flighting in the misty autumn sunrise.

About 20–30 pairs of greylag which had nested on the islands and neighbouring moorland of Loch Druidibeg during the summer, had produced as many fledged goslings, and these were augmented by about the same number of juveniles of the same stock, not yet paired. The whole flock roosted on Loch Druidibeg, and in the morning flew in noisy gaggles just above the crofthouse roofs to settle for the day in the stubbles and stooks from Dromore to Howmore. In those days this was the stronghold of the native greylag in Britian, and it was for this reason that the Reserve was created initially, with the breeding islands and neighbouring shores of Loch Druidibeg owned and managed by the Conservancy as a strict wildlife sanctuary. Since then, the special interest in the Reserve has been extended to include the entire succession of species and habitats from the sandy shore to the peat moorland. (It is a pity though that the boundaries were not extended to run from the western to the eastern shores of South Uist, thus encompassing the sheltered, rocky, weed-infested shores, without which a comprehensive nature reserve in the Outer Hebrides is incomplete.)

In a survey of 1968–72, Newton and Kerbes (1974) found some 60 pairs of greylag geese and less than 20 on nearby moorland, producing between 30 and 53 broods. Most of the broods hatched among the heather of the willow-, birch-, rowan- and juniper-wooded islets, and were soon on the loch after hatching. However, Loch Druidibeg itself with its heathery, sedgy margins has poor feeding for goslings compared with the rich green pastures beside the nearby machair lochs. Thus the broods were quickly led along the watercourses to Lochs Stilligarry and a'Mhachair, where they stayed until fledged.

During and after the last war, the native greylag stock were used to supplement the stocks of crofthouse birds with the eggs hatched under broody hens. Numbers of breeding pairs declined but nesting continued at Loch Druidibeg where they were accorded some protection by the estate, and a few pairs continued to breed in North Uist and Lewis.

In the past twenty-five years though, the picture has changed; the greylags are no longer concentrated in and around Loch Druidibeg. From that centre, and with the protection of the breeding sites afforded them there, they have colonised many of the inland loch-systems in the Uists and Benbecula. Currently there are 2,500–3,000 native greylag geese in Britain, with 500 to 700 breeding pairs (Owen *et al.*, 1986), of which 230–243 pairs (*c.* 1,860 birds of all ages) are in the Uist and Benbecula (Pickup, 1982), up to 30 are in the Sound of Harris, 10–15 are in Lewis, *c.* 15 are in the Summer Isles, 2–9 are in Coll, and one and two pairs are in Canna and Rum respectively (Thom, 1986). The main breeding concentration is now located on the loch-riddled landscape and east coast islands of North Uist. Paterson (1987) has updated the census in the Uists (Table 9), and estimated the breeding population as 156 pairs, which does not indicate a serious decline since 1982 because Pickup's data included unconfirmed reports, while Paterson's did not.

Island	February	August
North Uist	805	812
Benbecula	65	147
South Uist	301	336
Total	1,171	1,295

Table 8   The numbers and distribution of greylag geese in the Uists in 1986.

In winter, some of the native greylag may leave the Outer Hebrides, for example to Tiree and Islay, and those that remain are joined by migrants, possibly from north-west Scotland or Iceland. Flocks of up to 200 migrating greylags pass through the Hebrides, pitching onto headlands, off-shore islets and coastal marshes.

Over the turn of the century until the Second World War, South Uist held the main stock of geese wintering in the Hebrides, and the lodges at Grogarry and Askernish were in the midst of excellent wildfowling grounds. Guns were posted across the bent hills at right angles to the shore, awaiting skein upon skein of barnacle geese in their daily flights along the seaboard from roosts to feeding areas and back. There were also other shooting lines posted to intercept white-fronts and greylag flying into the stubbles and cattle pastures, and shooting of both geese and ducks from 'blinds' along the chain of machair lochs from Loch Bee to Loch Hallan. Then there were many thousands of barnacle and white-fronted geese but now there are only a few hundred of each species (Tables 6 and 8), more of the former than the latter. The main barnacle goose flocks in the Outer Hebrides are in the Barra Sound (*c.* 400), Monach Isles (*c.* 700), in Harris Sound (*c.* 1,200) and Shiant Islands (*c.* 500). The white-fronted geese have declined in numbers with only 70–80 in small flocks on South Uist remaining.

Swans

The Uists and Benbecula hold the main concentrations of swans in the Hebrides and are one of the densest breeding areas in Scotland, with over 20 pairs per sq km. Some 400 Mute swans (*Cygnus olor*), a moult flock of fully-grown, non-breeding birds, spend the summer on Loch Bee. The habitat is ideal—the shallow machair lochs and associated reed beds and marshes provide excellent nursery grounds. Mutes with collars attached at Loch Bee in 1979 have later been seen as far south as Kintyre and County Derry (Spray, 1982) and in Tiree between 1982 and 1987. They breed in small numbers in Barra, Tiree, Coll, Jura, Islay, and Gigha (Thom. 1986). In autumn, many hundreds of whooper swans (*Cygnus cygnus*) pass through the Hebrides from Iceland to Ireland, and we have spent some wonderful days on North Rona in October with swans (and geese) passing. At the other end of the Hebrides, at Balephuil, we often see the return April flight northward of whoopers. From Ireland they come in tight flocks just above the breakers, rise over the dune rampart and settle on the coastal lagoon of Loch a'Phuil, with much musical calling to and from the residents. In mid-October 1981, Chris Spray counted 359 whooper swans wintering in the Uists and Benbecula with probably about 450 in the Outer Hebrides as a whole. In the Inner Hebrides, the main whooper ground is in Tiree with 100–120 in January, and only a few birds on passage in Islay. A few well-separated whoopers, mostly with non-lethal injuries, spend the summer in the Hebrides. Pairs have bred successfully in Benbecula (1947) and Tiree (1977–9).

Ducks

Table 13.6 shows the distribution of breeding swans, geese and ducks in the Hebrides. Eider (*Somateria mollissima*), Mallard (*Anas platyrhynchos*) and red-breasted merganser (*Mergus serrator*) are the most numerous and most widely distributed of the ducks. The eider usually nests within easy distance of the sea or estuaries for transfer of small ducklings to rearing areas, and is absent from the interior of the largest islands—Lewis, Skye, Mull and Islay. The mallard and merganser breed throughout the islands, but not on the high hilltops and in the remote outliers—there are no breeding records of these species from St Kilda or North Rona. Shelduck are widespread in the Uists and Harris, and occur locally elsewhere, except in central and north Lewis where breeding has not been recorded. Where they occur together, eider are usually seen in tens and shelduck in pairs.

The breeding distributions and numbers of other species of duck are much more discontinuous than the foregoing, and with the exception of teal (*Anas crecca*) others are comparatively rare as breeders though common enough in passage or wintering. For example, wigeon, tufted duck (*Aythya fuligula*), pochard (*A. ferina*), pintail, (*Anas acuta*), gadwall (*A. strepera*) and shoveler (*A. clypeata*) breed mainly in North Uist. There are a few pairs of pintail and shoveler in South Uist, Benbecula and Tiree; and two old records of gadwall in Tiree and shoveler as an irregular breeder in Islay (Ogilvie, 1983; Ogilvie and Atkinson-Willes, 1983; Cunningham, 1983; Thom, 1986).

Island	\#Species of Wildfowl																	
	1	2	3	4	5	6	7	8	9	10	11	12	13	14	15	16	17	18
Lewis			+		+	+		+	*						*		*	
Harris			+		+			+	*						*		*	
North Uist	*		*		+	+	+	*	*	+	+	+	*	+	*		*	
Benbecula	*	+	*		+	+		*	*	+			*		*		*	
South Uist	*		*		+		+	*	*	+		+	*		*		*	
Barra	?				+			+	*						*		*	
Skye			+		+	+		+	*	o		+	+		*		*	+
Raasay									*						*		*	
Small Isles					+			+	*						*		*	
Coll	+		+		+	o		?	*						*		?	
Tiree	+	+			+	?	+	*	*	+	+	o	+		*	o	*	?
Mull	+				+				*				+		*		*	
Jura					+			+	*						*		*	
Islay	+				+			+	*				+		*	+	*	?
Colonsay				+	+			?	*				?		*		*	
Gigha	+				+	?		?	*				?		*		?	
Lismore	+								*						*		?	

* widespread   + scarce   ? possible breeder   o record before 1950

1 Mute swan   2 Whooper swan   3 Greylag goose   4 Canada goose   5 Shelduck   6 Wigeon   7 Gadwall   8 Teal   9 Mallard   10 Pintail   11 Shoveler   12 Pochard   13 Tufted duck   14 Scaup   15 Eider duck   16 Common scoter   17 Red-breasted merganser   18 Goosander

Table 9   Distribution of breeding swans, ducks and geese in the Hebrides, compiled from Hopkins and Coxon, 1979; Ogilvie, 1983; Ogilvie and Atkinson-Willes, 1983; Cunningham, 1983; Thom, 1986.

The Machair Islands

CHAPTER 5

Tiree and the Uists

About 6,600 years ago, when man first moved into the Hebrides, the islands had still to take on their present shape. The hard rock had already been moulded by the ice, but further changes in the shorelines were ahead. Drifts of gravel and sand, and deposits of peat, changed the appearance and nature of the islands. The natural history, land-use economy and culture of many of the islands on the outer fringe of the Hebrides from Lewis to Oronsay was greatly influenced by influxes of white, shell-sand from the sea which was blown inland to form a thick carpet on exposed western coasts. *Machair*, the Gaelic word for the grassland ecosystem which has formed on this sand, is uniquely apt, because nowhere else are there meadows quite like these. This grassy plain contrasts sharply with the generally dark, peaty and rocky interiors of the islands, and between the two the cottages of crofters and small farmers are often built. The machair also provides grazing for livestock and rich hay meadows in an otherwise agriculturally poor environment.

We have already given an account of the maritime system which results in the creation of machair (Ch. 6, H-ANT), and now we consider this environment; how it has evolved in relation to management by man and what it has to offer in both an aesthetic and a practical sense.

At 138m above sea level, the summit of Beinn Hynish is the highest point on Tiree. Yet, from this relatively low point (now holding a huge-domed radar station) there is a clear view to Barra, Skye, Mull, Islay and the horizon of the wide Atlantic broken only by the stack of the Skerryvore lighthouse. Tiree is the most remarkable machair island of all. It is 17km long by between 1–10km across, and shaped like a loin chop (Fig. 9). Mather, Smith and Ritchie (1975) have calculated that of the 77 sq km of land surface, 25.8 sq km (33.5%) consists of dunes and machair compared with 10% in South Uist. The remainder consists of 41.5% of raised beach surfaces (cultivation, heath and open water) and 25.0% of rock (bare rock, heath and open water).

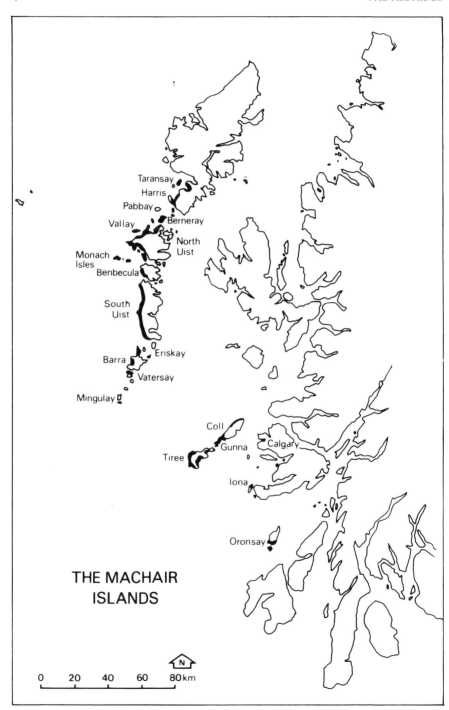

THE MACHAIR
ISLANDS

0   20   40   60   80 km

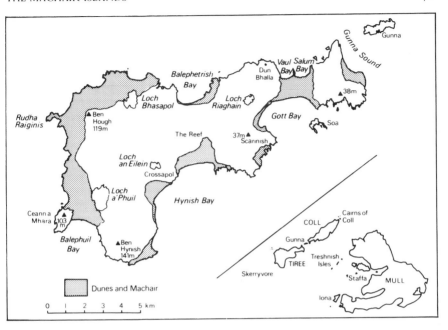

Fig. 9
Map of Tiree

One can see how the rocky ridge stretching from the Cairns of Coll to MacKenzie's Rock, 5km south-west of Skerryvore, must have presented a barrier over which ice from the Caledonian plateau moved with great force. The ice waxed and waned over the period of general retreat and ultimately disappeared, but there were adjustments to the level of the land and sea caused by loss of the ice burden (see Ch. 1, H-ANT for a description of the post-glacial isostatic uplift and sea level changes). This created the raised beaches of the Hebrides. Seventy-five per cent of Tiree is a raised tidal platform, strewn with glacial debris dropped by melting ice and later rearranged by the sea and wind. Much of the shell sand present in the Hebrides, which makes up most of the beach/dune/machair systems, is of ancient origin. During the post-glacial period, molluscs and crustacea were once abundant in the seas surrounding the Hebrides and it is the remains of the exoskeletons of these animals which account for a significant proportion of land in the Hebrides today. It is thought that little new sand is now being added and that localised erosion is balanced by localised accretion.

From Beinn Hynish the natural pattern of vegetation is obvious; the dark heathland of the rocky interior constrasting with the light, fresh greens of the machair grasslands and saltings by the shore. Hollows in the gneiss rock platform have given rise to small acid lochs, but Loch a'Phuil and Loch

Fig. 8
Location map of the machair islands, those islands which possess large amounts of shell sand in beaches and dunes and have machair grassland

Bhasapol, placed between the dunes and the hard core of the island, are alkaline machair lochs (see Ch. 10, H-ANT).

The dunes and machair have grown in parallel with human settlement of the islands; there are signs of wind-blown sand particles in intertidal peat at Borve on Benbecula from 5,700 years ago, and within the many layers of sand and debris laid down chronologically over the millenia, there are also the remains of human settlement. The five main interludes are Neolithic, Beaker, Iron Age, Viking/Medieval and Historical, and sites such as Rosinish on Benbecula, Udal on North Uist and Northton on Harris possess most if not all of these interludes of occupation. Other sites have the remains of Iron Age 'wheelhouses', under- and over-lain by blown sand. Such single-interlude sites are on low machair plains, while the multiple sites are on higher machair plains and hills. The wheelhouse sites are often waterlogged or collapsing at the front from coastal erosion.

The sandy drift is usually well stratified. Starting at the bedrock, there are usually several metres of layered sand and sandy soil. Each layer contributes to the record of ecological history; layers of pure sand indicate periods of windblown transgression of sand and instability of the land surface while organic soil indicates time of stability and growth of vegetation. If waterlogged at sometime these layers may be dark-coloured and peaty in texture. Staining may also arise from the water-table oscillating through the contact surfaces of peaty soils and white sand, thus causing the sand particles to become stained by the peaty water. Within these strata man's artifacts occur, and can be used to age different horizons in the sequence.

The Mesolithic sites in the Hebrides are not on machair because there was probably little or no machair about 6,500 years ago. The earliest inhabited sites on machair are Neolithic, situated on the glacial till, going back to about 5,800 BP and lasting until about 4,400 BP. These are overlain by Bronze Age (Beaker) occupations dated between 3,500 and 2,500 BP, which are in turn overlain by Iron Age occupations between about 2,500 and 1,500 BP. The uppermost strata are from the Viking/Medieval and historical periods when, in other parts of the islands, the beehive houses, duns and blackhouses were built in places where the soil was shallow and the country rock exposed. It is always fascinating to look at erosion faces in the machair dunes, especially in the lower dark layers of ancient organic soil, for ancient human litter such as shaped stones, fragments of pottery and bone, animal teeth, shells and, if lucky, pieces of flint. The complexity of machair soil sections is shown in Fig. 35 where those from Rosinish and Northton are shown (Ritchie, 1979).

Fig. 10
Machair stratigraphy—sections of machair soil at Rosinish, Benbecula and Northton, Harris showing the periods of human occupation (from Ritchie, 1979)

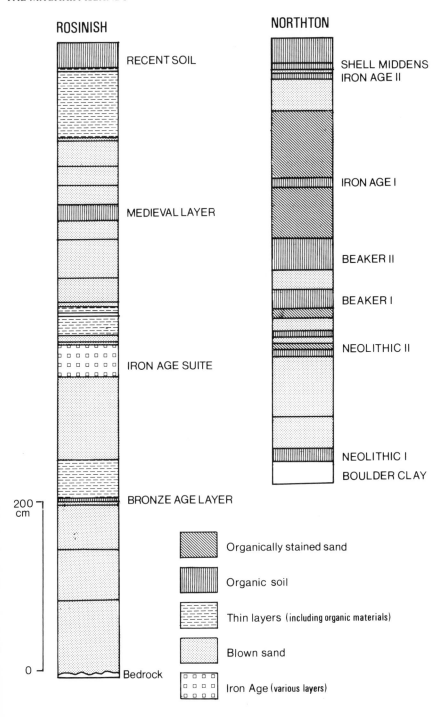

ROSINISH

RECENT SOIL

MEDIEVAL LAYER

IRON AGE SUITE

BRONZE AGE LAYER

200 cm

0

Bedrock

NORTHTON

SHELL MIDDENS
IRON AGE II

IRON AGE I

BEAKER II

BEAKER I

NEOLITHIC II

NEOLITHIC I
BOULDER CLAY

Organically stained sand

Organic soil

Thin layers (including organic materials)

Blown sand

Iron Age (various layers)

Dun Bhalla at Vaul,
Tiree showing the
internal diameter of
Iron-age dun/farm
now grass-covered, and
the surviving base of
the cavity wall into
which there is a low
entrance, in 1988
(Photo J. M. Boyd)

The history of Dun Bhalla the Iron Age fort-farm on Tiree is known in detail from the excavation and studies of Dr Euan Mackie. Tiree has a score or more of small forts which were constructed from the Iron Age into Viking times. They are thought to have served as defences against raiders, and were used by a pastoral people who herded their livestock and grew their crops on the machair. The people who lived in eastern Tiree at the time of Dun Bhalla were Iron Age farmers living in wooden homesteads. The Dun was built in the first century BC, probably by new settlers who brought with them stone-building craftsmen. It was built on a headland backed by spacious ranges of dunes, flats of machair and heath, some of which might have held scrub woodland. The excavation shows, however, that the 30ft high building survived for only about a century; in the second century AD it was much reduced in height, and converted into a farm. Tiree, for the time being at least, had come upon more peaceful times.

Returning to Beinn Hynish, the hill possesses three duns, several field systems of different occupations placed one upon another, stone alignments and green knolls suggesting ancient domestic or ceremonial sites, turf dykes, ruined blackhouse-type dwellings, and ditches from the time when the hill was cleared of cottars to create a large sheep farm at Hynish. The modern boundary dykes and fences mark the common grazings

Map showing the
distribution of machair
in the Uists and Barra
(from Ritchie, 1976)

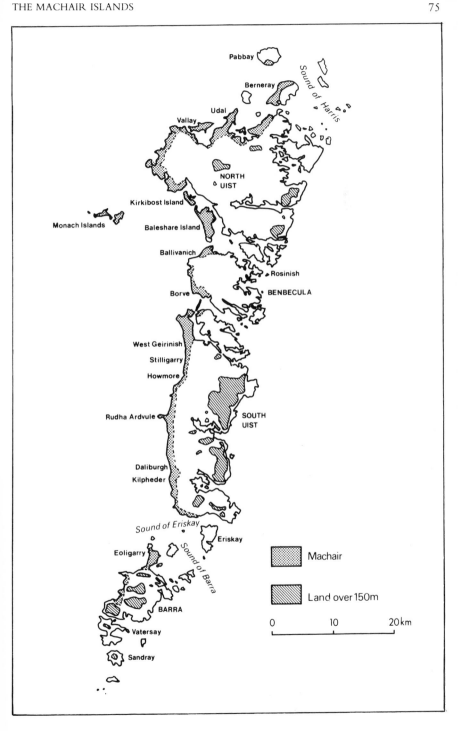

Pabbay

Berneray

Sound of Harris

Udal

Vallay

NORTH
UIST

Kirkibost Island

Monach Islands

Baleshare Island

Ballivanich

Rosinish

Borve

BENBECULA

West Geirinish

Stilligarry

Howmore

Rudha Ardvule

SOUTH
UIST

Daliburgh

Kilpheder

Sound of Eriskay

Eriskay

Eoligarry

Sound of Barra

BARRA

Vatersay

Sandray

Machair

Land over 150m

0   10   20 km

of five townships settled by crofters last century and managed today by their descendants. In the 6th century AD, Saint Columba arrived at Iona from Ireland and founded (563 AD) the monastery there. It was subsequently destroyed by the Vikings on five occasions between 795 and 986 AD, with the murder of the abbot and monks in 806, 825 and 986 AD. If such was the treatment of the monastery by Norsemen, one can imagine that the treatment of other island communities that possessed any wealth was no less drastic, though no record of such has survived. Tiree probably had a thousand years of agriculture before the arrival of the Columban monks, who regarded the island as Tir Iodh, the Land of Corn. In those far-off days of sail, there was a traffic directly between the isles which does not exist in today's jet age.

The machair islands have been grazed and cultivated since the first settlers arrived in the Hebrides. When grazing continues all year round, as happens when both rabbits and livestock are present, the pastures fail to flower and set seed. Eventually this depletes the swards of many species of plant, especially annuals, and encourages the spread of moss. It may also lead to thinning of the turf, opening the machair to the threat of erosion. However, since the machair ecosystem has evolved under the influence of grazing livestock, too little grazing can also be detrimental as it will lead to long and rank grass which provides little opportunity for annual herbs to survive. Occasionally, as in old hay meadows or in grazings used mainly for overwintering cattle, a balance is maintained between the potential degradation of the machair by erosion on the one hand and the loss of species diversity and productivity on the other. The best effects are seen where there are no rabbits, such as at The Reef on Tiree, or where the hay meadows are so close to the crofthouses, as at Kilpheder in South Uist, as to discourage rabbits. The rabbit-infested, overgrazed, wind-eroded south side of Ben Eoligarry in Barra is an object lesson in the amount of damage that can be done by rabbits and livestock but which, paradoxically, has the prettiest display of primroses in early June that we have seen anywhere.

The Monach Isles

If Tiree is the most remarkable of the larger machair islands, the Monach Isles fit the same description for the smaller islands. The first sight that many visitors to the Outer Hebrides have of the Monachs is from the passenger aircraft landing at Balivanich, Benbecula. They appear about 14km to the west in the lap of the ocean, while from the shore they are 12km distant

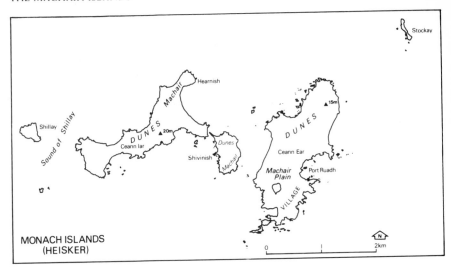

Fig. 12
Map of the Monach Islands

and appear as a rampart of pale sand dunes, above which rises the stalk of the disused lighthouse. It is understandable therefore, that the islands also carry the old Norse name Heisker, meaning Bright Rock; in the morning sunshine the cream-coloured sand-hills and the milk-white surf create an unmistakably bright impression. When ashore, the islands in summer are a blaze of flowers; daisies, bird's-foot trefoil, white clover, buttercups, eyebright, sea-pansies and many others. The Monach Isles, like Tiree, are emergent humps of gneiss, which are in this case tilted slightly to the west. The Monach platform was probably joined to North Uist before and during the postglacial adjustments of sea level. Now the depth between the islands is from 10–40m over a varied seabed of solid rock, boulders and sand. This shallow shelf is exposed to the full force of the Atlantic, and there is a build-up of breakers around the islands which absorbs energy from the swell before it reaches the shore of North Uist. It is on the outer reaches of this shelf that the power of the seas around the British Isles is at its greatest and where, at some future time, wave energy generators may be placed.

The Monach Isles (Fig. 12) consist of about 577 ha. of hummocked landscape, covered mostly by low dunes with high ridges, a machair plain with lochan and marshes plus sandy, pebbly and rocky shores with shingle ridges. The dunes are from 8–15m above sea level and the flat machair is less than 8m above sea level. There are two main islands, Ceann Ear ('East End', 193ha.) and Ceann Iar ('West End', 135ha.), joined at low tide by a sandy, tidal flat including the islet of Shivinish (28ha.). This group of three is separated from Shillay (16 ha.) by deeper water. Shillay, which has the lighthouse, and Stockay (3ha.) are both rocky. The little archipelago is 7.5km from east to west and 3km from north to south, and has been used for grazing live-stock, arable agriculture, fishing and probably also for the hunting of seals and seabirds.

Dean Monro wrote in 1549 that Heisker belonged to the Nuns of Columnkill, and there is a tradition of a nunnery on Shivinish and a monastery on Shillay where a beacon was maintained. Bleau's Atlas (1654) shows two places of worship on 'Hekskyr or Na Monich', and there is a record of a cargo of barley-meal being sent from Heisker to Ballachulish in 1692 for the starving and destitute MacIans following the massacre of Glencoe. The prosperity of the islands was confirmed by Martin in 1695, who mentions fertile soils, corn and black cattle. The Monach Isles had probably been settled for cen-turies, but are now deserted. There was probably once a crossing from Piable in North Uist to the Monach Isles, and the inhabitants left a legend that their last crossing of the land bridge was made about 1650 by a girl taking a heifer to a bull. This coincides with the tradition of the inundation by sea and sand of the island village of Baleshare on the neighbouring coast of North Uist.

In the late 19th century there was a 'run-rig' system (see pp. 113, H-ANT) of 10 crofts on Ceann Ear and the other two main islands were common grazings. The land was cultivated for three years with a rotation of barley, oats and potatoes. Seaweed was used as manure, and the land was then left fallow for several years. The crops were unfenced, so herdsmen kept the stock and at night animals were gathered and enclosed. For the remainder of the year they ranged freely. The land or 'scat' was sectioned in shares to each crofter who was also allocated a number of grazing animals ('souming') on the common. Corn was kiln-dried and milled in hand querns. The 'souming' in the 1930s for each of the three surviving crofter families was 8 cows, 2 horses and 24 sheep. Ceann Iar and Shivinish has no dry-weather freshwater supply, so cattle were therefore removed in summer while sheep grazed the islands all year round. There was no fuel, so peat was brought from North Uist and later coal was imported by the lighthouse tender. Cultivation ended in 1947, five years after the last family left.

Fishing was important in the economy of the community. Each family usually had a 10m open boat with sails and oars for fishing and to carry livestock, peats and merchandise. Fin-fish caught in summer were wind-dried and salted, and latterly there was creel fishing for lobsters and crabs. Periwinkles, bivalves and limpets provided food from the shore. Kelp (wind-dried wrack) was burnt in winter on simple hearths and the potash was exported in the spring. Now all this activity has ceased—although Heisker is still used for grazing sheep by a farmer from North Uist—and about 10 boats, mostly from Grimsay, work the lobsters, and the old schoolhouse is used as a bothy by the fishermen. The islands are owned by Countess Granville, except for Shillay which belongs to the Commissioners of the Northern Lighthouses. The entire group is a National Nature Reserve and Site of Special Scientific Interest managed jointly by the owners, tenants and the Nature Conservancy Council.

One of us (JMB) first went to the Monach Isles in the early 1960s from Gramsdale Benbecula, in an 8m open boat of a type used by Uist fishermen for a century or more—in fact the six-oared Highland boat which took Martin to Heisker and St Kilda in 1695 was probably an antecedent of this type of craft built in Grimsay. After navigating the sandy shallows of Oitir Mhor and breasting the ocean swell over the bar of Beul an Toim, our Grimsay skipper hoisted sail. In a lively, well-listed fashion, we made for Heisker; in the age of the power-boat this was a pleasure in itself and also a rerun of medieval history. For two hours we shared the wind with fulmars, terns, gulls, auks, gannets and cormorants, before landing at Port Ruadh with a more heightened sense of achievement than if we had been driven there by an engine-powered boat.

On going ashore, the place is alive with birds; gulls, terns, shelducks, eiders, red-breasted mergansers, oyster-catchers, ringed plovers, rock pipits, pied wagtails and starlings. Above the shore is the low eroded dune crest from which one can look across a flat machair plain to an encirclement of shaggy dunes. The succession of seaward and landward dunes, which we described in Chapter 6, H-ANT is absent on the Monach Isles due to their small size. The axes of the islands are roughly parallel with the prevailing south-west wind, which has probably caused the downwind sides of the islands to be blown clear of sand to form one of the finest ranges of dunes in the Hebrides, at the north end of Ceann Ear. These high dunes fill the landscape to the north of the machair plain with rock outcrops, upon which the scattered village ruins stand stark. Everywhere there are rabbit burrows and the occasional sprinkling of sturdy looking cattle, and the green meadows are misted with white and yellow daisies, wild white clovers, buttercups and trefoils.

Dr Roland Randall (1976) described seven main plant communities on the Monach Isles: (1) mobile dune with marram grass; (2) stable dune with marram and sand sedge; (3) flat dune with marram, sand sedge, daisy, ribwort and mosses; (4) machair with no marram but with sand sedge, daisy, red fescue, ribwort, plantain, yarrow, eyebright and lady's bedstraw; (5) sand-sedge pasture with red fescue, daisy, ragwort and yarrow; (6) sea pink sward with sea plantain, sea milkwort and red fescue (salting) and (7) peaty sedgeland with common sedge, white clover, red fescue, Yorkshire fog, marsh pennywort and silverweed (see also p. 102–103, H-ANT). Other more localised communities occur such as on the strand line with sea spurrey, sea arrow grass and salt-marsh grass; wet slacks have sedges, jointed rush and silverweed; fens have spike rush, mare's tail, sedges and cotton grass; Stockay has tall herb stands with cow parsnip; heaths have ling, creeping willow and devil's bit scabious; vegetated cobble has cleavers *Galium aparine* and the lochs have pondweeds, water milfoil and water crowfoot. The stands of undisturbed machair are rich in clovers, and the disturbed ground has much perennial rye grass. Perring and Randall (1972) have recorded 257 species of plant on the Monach Isles, and since then another has been found, the rue-leaved saxifrage (*Saxifraga tridactylites*). Other species of special note are the oyster plant (*Mertensia maritima*), adder's tongue (*Ophioglossum vulgatum*), field gentian (*Gentianella campestris*), water whorl-grass (*Catabrosa aquatica*), small sweet grass (*Glyceria declinata*) and the greater tussock-sedge (*Carex paniculata*). The black oat (*Avena strigosa*) is a relict cultivar and the northern marsh yellow-cress (*Rorippa islandica*), which is a common plant of the summering grounds of the barnacle goose in the Arctic, is also present in this, one of the Scottish wintering grounds. Other northern species are also found on the Monach Isles; for example the oyster plant, which is a northern species, grows beside the southern bog pimpernel, and similarly, continental species such as the mountain everlasting, water dropwort and the frog orchid occur in an otherwise oceanic community.

The ruined village is situated at the southern end of the machair plain close to the lochs. In 1815 about 100 people and 1,000 cattle and sheep were thought to have lived on the Monach Isles, but this was reduced to one family in the early 20th century. However, recovery was quick, because by 1846 there were 39 inhabitants, and by 1867 there were between 80 and 90 with 75 on Ceann Ear, this number remaining static until the 1914–18 War. In 1886 there were 8 crofter and 6 cottar families, and about the turn of the century there were about 60 children at school. The crofter families lived in clusters of buildings including house and steadings enclosed in a stack yard, whereas the cottars had solitary cottages, and were probably squatters eeking out an existence in fishing, beach-combing for shell-fish, kelp burning and helping crofters. By the mid-1920s there were 10 families, and in 1939 only two remained, those of John and Alexander MacDonald, plus the lightkeepers. In 1942 the lighthouse was closed, and in 1943 the MacDonalds left. During the period 1942–49 the family of Peter Morrison of Grimsay lived on Ceann Ear, but after this the Monach Isles had no permanent inhabitants.

Machair—A Natural Heritage

The machair islands are valued pieces of Britain's natural heritage which have seen large changes in the last two centuries. The human population was greatest on the machair islands between 1821 and 1841; in 1831 there were 4,453 inhabitants on Tiree compared with 760 in 1981, similarly, in 1821, 4,971 people lived on North Uist, but by 1981 the total was 1,670. There was a similar decline on South Uist although numbers there have been kept high by the presence of army personnel. The height of the population coincided with the peak of the kelp industry, and followed the reorganisation of estates. In some of these estates many small tenancies, involving runrig cultivation and common grazings with houses in clusters, were changed to crofts with enclosed arable land, common grazings and houses well separated on the enclosed land. By 1830, however, the kelp industry was waning, the estates were in poor financial straits and the population was far in excess of the islands' resources. On Benbecula and South Uist, the land that had not been assigned to crofts was cleared, and the clearances of tacksmen (leasees) and cottars (sub-tenants or squatters) continued when the estates passed from Clanranald to the Gordons of Cluny in 1838. Poverty was rife, and many cottar families emigrated to Canada and Australia.

At this time agricultural improvement took on a new pace, with a subsequent loss of parts of the machair and hill-grazings of the crofting township to extend new farms. By 1850, nine-tenths of the population was concentrated on less than one-third of the land of South Uist, and it was at this time that the main drains were dug that no doubt changed the character of the wetlands. Later, the Crofters' Act of 1886 gave security of tenure to the crofter-tenants, and in 1897 the Congested Districts Board was empowered to resettle or encourage estates to resettle crofters on farms. Thus by 1924 those lands that had been largely cleared of tacksmen and cottars were apportioned into crofts and resettled. The present crofting pattern of land-tenure dates from about the 1820s, but was not complete until about the 1920s. In the past 30 years, many machairs, which had been common land for cultivation and grazing, have been apportioned to individual crofts, fenced and cultivated.

The influence of this turbulent socio-economic history on the wildlife of the machair islands is unrecorded. However, there are accounts which indicate that at times of high human population the machair grasslands may have become extensively unstable, and drifted into dunes. About 1811 James Macdonald wrote of South Uist and Barra:

In winter, and even until the middle of May, the western division or machair, is almost a desolate waste of sand; and this sand encroaches rapidly the next division, namely that of lakes and that of firm arable ground.

Also, describing the Monach Isles about 1815 Captain Otter stated,

the whole surface of Ceann Ear (the main arable land) was denuded of soil.

These descriptions are probably exaggerated, but it is almost certain that the socio-economic changes of the times were accompanied by some ecological changes which have contributed to the consitution of the valued machair habitats of today. The fact that many of the features of the machair result from human activity over the centuries does not detract from its value as a habitat for wildlife; most landscapes in Britain have a significant man-made component, and the modern attitude is that the human component is often not at all bad. In fact, some habitats are so far from being natural (i.e. unaffected by man) that it is positively detrimental to the wildlife they contain to allow them to look after themselves. To retain floristic variety, grasslands such as machair often require moderate grazing, and many of the stages between arable and ley provide fine mosaics of wild flowers and nesting sites for waders and songbirds. Cultivation and heavy grazing or rabbit-infested machairs on the other hand can cause widespread blowing sand in place of pasture. Deep drainage lowers the water table, makes the dry dunes drier, shrinks the machair lochs and dries out dune slacks, marshes and fens, all rich in wetland flowers, waders and wildfowl. Reseeding and the use of concentrated fertilisers and herbicides on old pastures, eliminates the highly diverse mixture of grasses, sedges and tall herbs. The wildlife of the machair has been created and maintained by traditional crofting agriculture, so it follows that large-scale changes in crofting can carry with them corresponding changes in the wildlife.

Most of the population of the corncrake (*Crex crex*) breeding in Britain, nests in the Hebrides, and it has become the symbol of conservation among the crofts of the machair islands. When the birds arrive in spring, they find cover in the early growth of yellow iris from which they move to nest in the young stands of barley, oats and hay ideal for them and their chicks. The cutting of the crops does not generally start until late July when the young are already mobile and able to avoid the mower, and in most cases, the hay meadows are alongside the strands of cereals or have marshy margins with iris, meadowsweet and common reeds which provide excellent escape cover for the crakes. Tiree has some of the finest corncrake habitat, and in the gloaming of a July day, a walk along any township road guarantees the sound of calling corncrakes from the dewy hay, barley, irises and reeds, the ratchety voice of the bird belying its beauty of shape and plumage (see pp. 131–4).

The distribution of machair in the Hebrides is seen in Fig. 33, which also shows the spot distribution of SSSIs containing machair habitat. The Integrated Development Programme (IDP) in the Outer Hebrides, which saw investment in agriculture, has, perhaps predictably, run its course without significant damage to the machair. However, it provided the stimulus for a flurry of research activity in 1983, when predictions of doom for the machair in the wake of updated agricultural practices, were rife. The concern which this created and the surveys which accompanied it has resulted in an enormous increase in our knowledge of the machair flora and fauna and their relationship to agricultural practice. In 1982–85 the NCC, with the support of the Environmental Directorate of the EEC and the co-operation of the RSPB, Wader Study Group, SWT and others, carried out a study of the environment implications of the IDP, and the results are contained in a tri-partite report *Agriculture and Environment in the Outer Hebrides* (Hambrey, 1986) and numerous separate published papers. An Agricultural Development Plan is now in progress in the Inner Hebrides, and much of the knowledge and experience gained in the IDP, particularly in the interactions of agriculture with nature conservation in crofting areas, will accrue to this new scheme.

CHAPTER 6

Rum—An Island Nature Reserve

The road to the isles immortalised in song runs 'by Ailort and by Morar to the sea'; it is effectively the A830 between Fort William and Mallaig, and the trail of tourists and fish-freezer juggernauts. Where the road turns sharply west at the high point at Back of Keppock there is a serene view; the western skyline holds the cuillins of both Skye and Rum, and often this is the traveller's first sight of the isles.

The centre piece is Rum (10,684ha.) which, as the drive proceeds north to Mallaig, gradually appears from behind the heights of Eigg and then stands proud of all other land, an elegant sweep of peaks blocking sight of Canna and the Uists. For a long time it was called the 'forbidden island', partly because of its sad history of clearance of its native Gaelic people in the 1820s when the island was owned by the Maclean of Coll, and partly because of the exclusive use of the island by the three wealthy familes who owned Rum from 1847–1957. They used the island as a sheep run, and after reintroducing red deer from 1845, as a sporting estate. Access between the mailboat and the island was by the owner's private boat, and the island afforded no inn to the casual visitor. Since 1957, when Rum was purchased as a National Nature Reserve by the Nature Conservancy, the ferry between the mainland and the island is still operated by the owner who also provides accommodation and campsites for visitors. Though visitors now make bookings for lodgings, increasing numbers arrive from yachts and tripper-boats from Mallaig and Arisaig, and none are turned away. Though certain restrictions have been applied in the interests of wildlife research and management over the last 30 years by the Nature Conservancy and its successors since 1973, the Nature Conservancy Council, the island is now far from being 'forbidden'. Indeed the *bona fide* visitor is invariably welcomed and asked to observe the rules which make the island available to people, without loss or damage to wildlife.

From Mallaig, Rum resembles an oceanic volcano whose shape speaks of wild and rugged scenery, and whose texture

appears sometimes gentle, and sometimes hard and sharp. In fact, Rum is an eroded Tertiary volcano and the other Small Isles are built mainly of lava and ash. The great magma chambers and vents of Rum have thrust their way through the existing crust of Mesozoic and Palaezoic rocks, and subsequently have been shattered and eroded by ice, sea and weather over tens of millions of years. What now remains are the cold, solid innards of the volcano, consisting mostly of basic (gabbro) and ultra-basic (peridotites and allivalites) igneous rocks within a frame of much older Torridonian sandstone, part of which is under the sea to the west.

As the mailboat crosses the Sound of Rum, the visitor becomes aware of the awesome character of the island — gone is the gentle, distant silhouette and in its place is the massive,

Rum ponies at the Bullough Mausoleum in Glen Harris, Rum. A small herd (c. 25) of ponies run wild on Rum, but are selectively bred and some are used to bring deer carcases off the hill (Photo J. M. Boyd)

wild reality of Rum. The lower half of the Rum cuillin shows
the dark-red Torridonian frame and the upper half, the dark-
grey basic and ultra-basic core. It has the scenic grandeur and
general ecology of the bare, deer-forest country of the north-
west Highlands, but it is more varied because of its unusually
wide range of rocks and soils, its responses to sea spray and
weather, and to the presence of 116,000 pairs of Manx shearwaters nesting in the mountain tops.

At the landing place in Loch Scresort, Rum rises steeply
from the village of Kinloch to the summit of Hallival (723m)
which leads to the summit of the island, Askival (812m). The

Fig. 13
Location map of Rum

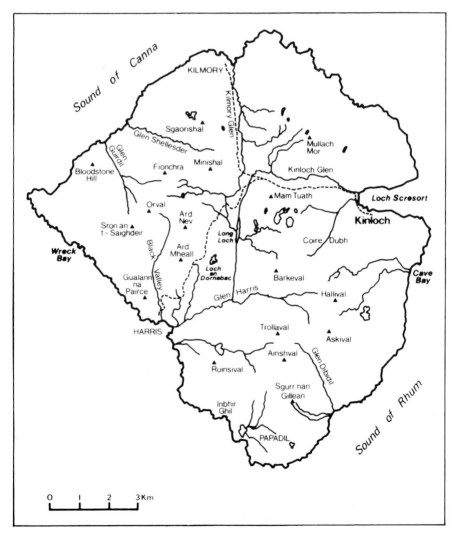

cluster of cottages in the wooded precincts of Kinloch Castle are today's statement of human habitation and landuse which goes back to prehistory, while the panoramic view from the top of Askival is unsurpassed for its inner whorl of surrounding peaks, and its mountainous and island-spattered outer circumference. Here, the naturalist with an eye for country can see an exciting field of exploration; the Inner Hebrides merge with the mainland massifs and the Outer Hebrides stand aloof, but each island is a microcosm awaiting discovery. Rum is now the most celebrated of them all as a centre of research, and one of the best documented islands in Britain. The vegetation and flora have been described by Eggeling (1965) and Ferreira (1967), the insects by Steel and Woodraffe (1969) and Wormell (1982), birds by Bourne (1957) and Love (1984), red deer by Clutton-Brock, Guinness and Albon (1982) and geology by Emeleus (1980). Also, a natural history of Rum has recently been edited by Clutton-Brock and Ball (1987).

The human history of Rum has been told by John Love (1983, 1987) and probably starts with the Mesolithic hunter-fishermen of about 6,600 years BC. There is a charcoal hearth and shell/bone midden at Bagh na h-Uamha (Caves Bay), in a situation characteristic of that used by these earliest settlers. That was in the Atlantic period when the climate was as moist as it is today, but over 2°C warmer. Rum was probably clad in a wild mixed forest on the lower ground from sea level up to 200m, dense on the sheltered side, and thin on exposed faces. There was probably a thinning of the forest on to the higher ground without a definite treeline, and the high tops were probably as clear of trees then as they are today. Without any appreciable human effect, the character of the maritime forest and heath would reflect solely the influence of natural factors of wind-blow, drainage, salt-spray, fire by lightening and the browsing and grazing of red deer and invertebrates. The ancient fauna may have become isolated there when the land and ice bridges disappeared at the end of the Quaternary ice age 10,000 years ago, or it may have arrived on rafts of storm-swept timber in which the sea and shores probably abounded. The field mouse, brown rat and pygmy shrew may have reached Rum naturally on such flotsam, but they may have come first by boat, possibly in Viking times (Berry, 1983); the pipistrelle bat probably reached the island naturally. This vision of the pristine state of the island is not just an idle dream; it is important to bear in mind when coming to decide the objects of management of Rum today, as a nature reserve.

The history of Rum therefore is a *vignette* of the Hebrides as a whole since the time of the first settlers; it plumbs the depths of human history in Scotland and holds the relics of successive cultures, while its rocks and soils range from the acid to the ultra-basic and the entire span of geological age from the Palaezoic to Recent. Its ecology embraces habitats from the very exposed to the sheltered and from the sea shore to the mountain tops, and it has it own unique inventory of plants and animals bound in a discrete ecosystem. Few small islands in Europe are more attractive to the naturalist than Rum as a nature reserve and a base for ecological research.

The Volcano

The Rum volcano dates back to the early Tertiary (Palaeocene) when, some 60 million years ago, Greenland and Europe began to drift apart and a great deal of volcanic activity occurred in north-west Britain (p. 24, H-ANT). The volcano was probably once a conical pile of cinder and lava possessing erupting craters and many NW-SE fissures which issued lava over about 10 million years. There were two main periods of eruption: the first predated the central volcano, and its relics occur in Eigg, Muck, and eastern Rum around Allt nam Ba and Beinn nan Stac; the second postdates the centre, and its relics are found in western Rum in Orval, Bloodstone Hill and Fionchra, and in Canna and Sanday. In the ensuing 50 million years, about 1km of the overburden has been removed by erosion which was very severe in the four ice-ages of the Pleistocene (c. 600,000 to 10,000 years ago). It was then that the island as we know it today was created, firstly as a *nunatak* protruding above the vast ice-sheet covering NW Europe, and later, when the ice melted, as a marine island in an arctic sea. Rum was probably high enough to have its own glaciers, which in the latter stages of the glaciation served to push aside the on-coming massive ice from the Caledonian plateau to gouge the valleys now drowned by the Sounds of Eigg, Rum and Canna. The cover having been stripped away, the roots of the volcano are again laid bare to the atmosphere in a complex of rocks and volcanic structures, affording a generation of geologists an unending field of study.

The oldest rock on Rum is the gneiss in the vicinity of the Priomh Lochs, and the massifs of Ainshval and Sgurr nan Gillean. Though the contact between the gneiss and the Torridonian sandstone usually indicates an Archaen land surface (see p. 33), the outcrop of the former is extraordinary. Because of volcanic activity, most of the gneiss is placed out of context within the ring fault which encircles most of the intrusive rocks in the roots of the volcano. Such a land surface probably exists under the Torridonian sandstone which occupies the northern

Fig. 14
*Geological map of Rum
(from Emeleus, in
Clutton-Brock and
Ball, 1987)*

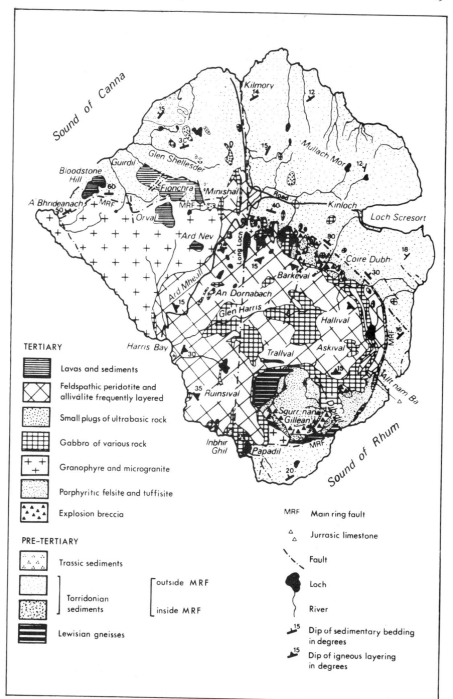

TERTIARY

	Lavas and sediments
	Feldspathic peridotite and allivalite frequently layered
	Small plugs of ultrabasic rock
	Gabbro of various rock
	Granophyre and microgranite
	Porphyritic felsite and tuffisite
	Explosion breccia

PRE-TERTIARY

	Trassic sediments
	Torridonian sediments [outside MRF / inside MRF]
	Lewisian gneisses

MRF   Main ring fault

△ △   Jurrasic limestone

   Fault

   Loch

   River

15   Dip of sedimentary bedding in degrees

15   Dip of igneous layering in degrees

and eastern parts of the island (Fig. 14). Between the old Torridonian and the young Tertiary rocks which make up the bulk of the island, there are middle-aged Triassic sediments which have been derived from the weathering of the Torridonian in a distant era of erosion. These are the sandstones and limestones—'cornstones'—of Monadh Dubh, and similar rocks of Jurassic age occur at Dibidil and Beinn nan Stac.

The much younger volcanic intrusion occupies the whole of the south-western sector, and is separated from the volcanic rocks by a complex ring fault that takes a convoluted course from Camus na h-Atha near Bloodstone Hill through Orval to the Kinloch-Kilmory-Harris watershed and from thence in a rough semi-circle through Meall Breac, Cnapan Breaca, Dibidil and Papadil. The emplacement of the granophyre of Orval and Ard Nev and other structures (felsite plugs, explosion breccias, tuffisites, basalt dykes and sills) came before the ring fault, but the ultrabasic and gabbros occurred afterwards, cutting and metamorphosing the existing rocks along the line of the fault. The structure, growth and decay of the volcano is described by Emeleus (1983, 1987).

The ultrabasic rocks of Hallival and Askival are well known for their layered appearance; they look like 'bedded' sedimentary rocks. This is caused, it is thought, by injections of magma into deep chambers of the volcano. Some of this magma would be expelled and some retained at intervals of time which allowed for very slow cooling and separation of heavy and light minerals. The residue of each injection is represented by a layer, the lower part of which is rich in denser, faster-settling olivine and the upper part in feldspar. Thus in a sequence of partial eruptions of the contents of the magma chambers, fifteen layers of thickness varying from 50 to 150m have been formed.

The Forest

A main objective of the nature reserve is to recreate a habitat resembling that which existed in Rum before the island was made treeless by man, and to achieve this, the managers must have a reliable picture of the island as it was 2,500 years ago at the beginning of the Iron Age. This has been done by the study of pollen and plant remains from bogs. Following the clearance of the ice in the Boreal period (10,000–7,000 BP) a forest of birch, pine, willow, hazel and juniper occupied the sheltered glens and slopes, and the glades and open range held bog myrtle, sedges, grasses and club mosses. The following period until 2,500 BP saw the climatic optimum, with maximum forest

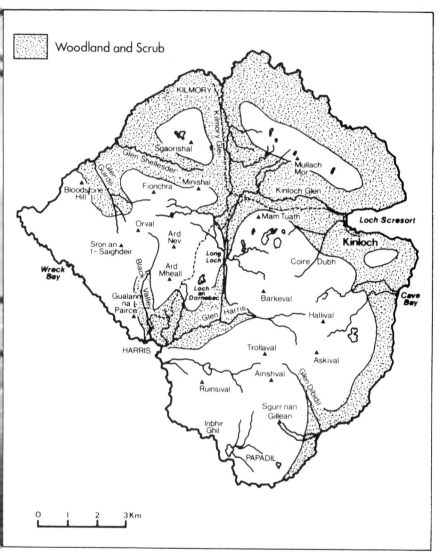

Woodland and Scrub

KILMORY

Sgaorishal

Glen Shellesder

Glen Guirdil

Bloodstone Hill

Fionchra

Minishal

Kilmory Glen

Mullach Mor

Kinloch Glen

Mam Tuath

Loch Scresort

Orval

Ard Nev

Kinloch

Sron an t-Saighdeir

Long Loch

Coire Dubh

Black Valley

Ard Mheall

Wreck Bay

Loch an Dornabac

Barkeval

Gualann na Pairce

Glen Harris

Hallival

Cave Bay

HARRIS

Trollaval

Askival

Ruinsival

Ainshval

Glen Dibidil

Sgurr nan Gillean

Inbhir Ghil

PAPADIL

0   1   2   3 Km

cover including oak, ash, alder, rowan and wych elm. The
maximum extent of the primaeval forest is shown in Fig. 15
(after Ball, 1987).

When the Iron Age people were rearing their stock around
Dun Bhalla in Tiree, others were settled in Rum and busy felling and burning the forest to make way for their livestock. At
the same time the climate became cooler and wetter with a
sharp increase in bog moss, bracken, alder, willow and juniper
and a decrease in oak and wych elm. Such fluctuations had

Fig. 15
*Forest map of Rum
(from Ball, in
Clutton-Brock and
Ball, 1987)*

taken place before 2,500 BP, but then there had not been
farmers with metal axes! The long-term decline of the forest
had begun, and was assisted on its way by the Norse invasion of
the 8th century. Felling, burning, grazing and cultivation continued and by medieval times the island was almost treeless. It
is clear that the medieval people of Rum had no sense of the
forest as a vital resource of shelter for stock, a source of timber
for fuel and for building houses and boats.

The peak human population on Rum was about 400, and
occurred in the early 19th century (Love, 1987) when there must
have been only a very few trees remaining, in inaccessible gullies. After the last copse was felled in 1796 (Ball, 1987), a tree
must have been a curio to the native-born Rumach; something
worth walking far to see. The island remained treeless for
about 50 years until, in the 1850s, the new owners planted the
large sycamores, beeches and elms which stand today behind
the Post Office on the site of the old Kinloch House (now
demolished). Plantations were extended around Kinloch
Castle and Loch Scresort in the early years of this century. Following an assessment of these woods Martin Ball states:

Altogether 120 tree species have been catalogued (for Rum) and,
though the woods do not resemble the natural forest, they have en-
abled many woodland plants to survive, including attractive carpets of
bluebell, wood sorrel and buckler fern, and many species of epiphytic
lichen and moss which depend on shade and high humidity. Some
more local woodland plants, including wood anemone and wood
sedge are now extinct outside the Kinloch woods.

In 1958, following the declaration of Rum as a National Nature
Reserve, the current reafforestation of the island was begun,
with the removal of sheep and the setting-up of small, deer-
fenced plantations in Kinloch, Kilmory and Harris Glens,
Guirdil, and in 1,400ha. of the sandstone hills to the north and
south of Loch Scresort.

Since 1960 well over half a million trees of 20 different
species have been raised in a nursery at Kinloch and established out of reach of deer and other livestock. Native trees of
West Highland stock—pine, birch, alder, ash, oak, wych elm,
rowan, aspen, willows, holly, bird cherry, hawthorn,
blackthorn, whin and broom—were planted on the ploughed
and unploughed land and given rock phosphate fertiliser in
moorland habitats most favourable to each. In habitats exposed
to high winds and salt spray, lodgepole pine (*Pinus contorta*)
from North America was used as a 'nurse' for the native trees.
Unfortunately, early growth was retarded by a fire which swept
through north-east Rum in March 1969, but the ecology of the
plantations is now greatly different to that of the open hill. After

25 years of respite from grazing, and the subsequent growth of trees, there are now extensive new woodland and moorland communities of native species which have been unrepresented on Rum for many centuries.

Already a woodland flora is shyly making its presence felt under the young trees where once there was heather and moor grass—honeysuckle; hard, mountain and buckler ferns; wavy and tufted hair grasses; bluebell; angelica; wood sorrel; primrose; wood violet; self heal, pignut; germander speedwell and blaeberry (Ball, 1987). When Rum lost its forest it also lost its woodland fauna, that assemblage of diverse creatures each specialised for life in one or more of the vast number of nooks and crannies of the forest. It is impossible to create an 'instant' flora and fauna for the new woodlands—such a thing has to develop in time; for example many insects live on dead wood, which in nature is usually provided by old, decaying trees, of which there are as yet few on Rum. However, since the first woods were established at Kinloch 80 years ago, 20 species each of arboreal Heteroptera and aphids and over 130 species of moth—the caterpillars of which feed on trees or shrubs—have been recorded. There are also many gall-forming sawflies, wood-boring beetles including the long-horn (*Asemum striatum*), ichneumon flies including the persuasive burglar (*Rhyssa persuasoria*), which is the parasite of the giant woodwasp *Uroceros gigas*. One leaf-miner moth (*Phyllonorycter maestingella*) on Rum has as many as six ichneumon parasites, showing how advanced the colonisation of the woodlands have become. The northern winter moth, which has flightless females, is also present, indicating perhaps that there has been sufficient woody habitat in the past to maintain a population (Wormell, 1987).

One-hundred-and-ninety-four species of bird have been recorded on Rum, of which 87 have bred on the island and over 50 now do so regularly (Love and Wormell, 1987). The Common Bird Census of 1974 found 23 species breeding in the mature woods around Kinloch: woodcock (2 pairs), common sandpiper (1), woodpigeon (10), collared dove (6), cuckoo (3), grey wagtail (2), pied wagtail (1), wren (18), dunnock (14), robin (43), blackbird (28), song thrush (17), mistle thrush (2), willow warbler (28), goldcrest (21), spotted flycatcher (1), long-tailed tit (6), coal tit (7), blue tit (9), treecreeper (4), hooded crow (2), house sparrow (6) and chaffinch (43). With the growth of the young plantations in recent years, this woodland community has been augmented in numbers, and by a few pairs each of whinchat, grasshopper warbler, whitethroat, garden warbler, wood warbler, chiffchaff, greenfinch, siskin, bullfinch and reed bunting. The blackcap may also breed there.

The recreation of the forest habitats of Rum is therefore well on its way, but will require to continue for many decades and to be extended westward into the glens of Kinloch, Kilmory and Shellesder. The grand vision of wild and mountainous Rum to some extent restored to its former wooded state, with the return of much of its wildlife naturally regenerating after centuries of deprivation, may not yet be an idle dream.

Red Deer

It was Fraser Darling who in 1933 first saw the scientific challenge in the study of red deer (*Cervus elaphus*) in the Scottish Highlands and Islands. Rum was his first choice as a centre for his deer study but Sir George Bullough, then the laird, refused him permission, and he carried out his pioneer research in Wester Ross. As if in posthumous irony to Sir George, who died in 1939, the Deed transferring Rum from the Bullough Family to the Nature Conservancy as a National Nature Reserve in 1957 bore the signature of F. Fraser Darling (as a member of the Conservancy). It therefore took over 20 years for the work he had started at Dundonnell (so well described in *A Herd of Red Deer*) to be recommenced by a succeeding generation of researchers, this time on Rum!

The life history of red deer has been traditional knowledge in the Highlands for centuries. In Scotland the red deer was originally an inhabitant of the forest, as it is today in continental Europe. However, as the Caledonian forest was destroyed progressively over many centuries from the Iron Age onwards, the red deer were probably reduced in numbers, and became well adapted for survival in the bare, almost treeless mountain country. Following the breakdown of the clan system after the Risings of 1715 and 1745, the clearance of the remaining forest and cottar communities to make way for sheep in the late 18th and early 19th centuries, and the establishment of the large sporting estates in the 18th and 19th centuries, the deer became more and more of a sporting asset to the landowner. In ancient times, the deer were hunted in the forest with bow and arrow and on the open hill by driving them into traps, and later, on the estates before the days of the rifle, deer-hounds were used to pursue and kill the deer. After the introduction of the rifle, the entire style of hunting was changed to stalking and killing of selected individuals. Stags possessing fine antlers (12 tynes is 'royal', 14 'imperial' and 0, 'hummel') became prize animals sought after by stalkers as 'trophy heads', so in a historical sense, the stalkers employed by the estates and their employers were the first paid observers of red deer. It was their traditional

knowledge as part of the lore of the Highlands that fired
Cameron to write *The Wild Red Deer of Scotland* (1923), and
Fraser Darling, as one of the first Leverhume Research Fel-
lows, to carry the work into the era of modern science in 1933.

*Rutting stag in Rum
(Photo T. H. Clutton-
Brock)*

On Rum the loss of forest and the increase in people and
domesticated stock (cattle, goats and ponies, as well as sheep)
resulted in the extermination of red deer in the 1780s. A flint
arrowhead found on Hallival indicates that deer may have been
hunted there in Stone Age times, and in Glen Duian there is a
deer trap similar to that described by Dean Monro in 1549,
which may have been used by the people in Glen Harris in
medieval times. Red deer were reintroduced to Rum in 1845
after the ownership of the island passed from the Maclean of
Coll to Lord Salisbury, and later to a Campbell family (Love,
1980). Further introductions of English park deer took place
later, to 'improve the stock' on Rum and the Bulloughs, who
acquired the island from the Campbells in 1886, maintained
the deer population between 1,200 and 1,700, and culled
annually some 40 each of stags and hinds. When the island

passed to the Nature Conservancy in 1957, sheep were removed and the deer population was held at a level of about 1,500, with a one-sixth cull of both stags and hinds. However, it was not found possible to maintain such a level of cull on Rum, where there is no recruitment from neighbouring unculled estates. Culls ranging from one-seventh to one-tenth of the population in April proved more appropriate, depending on the size of the population. On the mainland where immigration is possible between estates, the experience and results gained from the one-sixth cull on Rum were later employed by the Red Deer Commission (Annual Reports 1961–75) in their advice to deer-forest managers throughout Scotland.

The seasonal rituals of stags and hinds take place on Rum as they do in all other deer forests. There are five different designated sectors of the population, with little exchange of hinds but much exchange of stags during the rut (p. 95). One of these sectors, the North Block, has been kept quiet and free from culling since 1972. In 1971 there were 60 hinds over one year old in this block and by 1983 that number had increased to 179. Stag numbers remained constant at 130 until 1980, when they decreased to 97 in 1983. In the ten-year study only two hinds left the block despite the reduction of the population in the neighbouring blocks by culling, though some on the edges of the block wandered further afield without becoming detached. As their numbers increased above 15 hinds per sq km, so the age at which hinds first conceived a calf changed from two to three years and the percentage of calving by 'milk' hinds (with a calf of the year at foot) dropped from 80 to 40%. Winter mortality of calves increased greatly from about 5 to about 35% of the total number of calves born in the previous summer. This resulted in a fall in the calf/hind ratio from 50 to 25 calves per 100 hinds.

As hinds increased, so the date of the rut became later and the performance of stags became affected. Stags were predisposed more to the stresses of high densities of hinds and accompanying food shortage than the hinds themselves. As hind numbers increased so the mortality of male calves and knobbers (male yearlings) rose more rapidly than in females, and growth of young males was more retarded than in females. In adult stags the mean age at death of those surviving for over three years fell from 14 to 10 years, while that of hinds remained constant between 12 and 14 years. The sex-ratio is therefore changed with an increasing bias in favour of hinds, proving that it is unwise to increase the number of hinds in order to provide a sustained stock of large stags. High stocks of hinds are associated with low performance of stags resulting in higher stag mortality and poor antlers (Fig. 16). Paradoxically, this goes

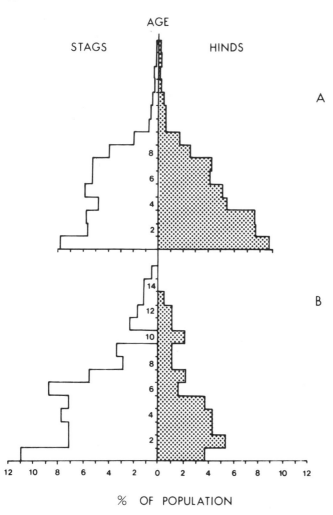

Fig. 16
*(a) Year class
percentages in the red
deer population of Rum
on 1st June 1957
reconstructed from
subsequent deaths and
estimated survivors up
to May 1966. (b)
Percentages of animals
in different year classes
in the North Block (of
Rum) in 1971 (from
Clutton-Brock,
Guinness and Albon,
1982)*

against the grain of traditional management of deer forests, where hind densities are allowed to increase to well in excess of optimal levels.

We have described this mechanism of natural control of deer numbers in some detail so as to convey an impression of the intricacy of the process and the finery of the research which has been done by the Large Mammal Research Group of Cambridge University — the full body of which is described by the principals Tim Clutton-Brock, Fiona Guinness and Steve Albon in *Red Deer: behaviour and ecology of two sexes* (1982), and *Red Deer in the Highlands* (1989), which are the very worthy successors to Fraser Darling's *A Herd of Red Deer* (1937), and which have a world-wide significance in the fields of population ecology and sociology in large herbivores.

Over 15 years the research team in the North Block has studied the entire lifespan of many individual deer in both sexes, and the build-up and decay of social groups. Hinds occur in groups of up to twenty related deer; each group having a matriarchy lead by old hinds and possessing kindred females and immature stags. The juvenile hinds remain with their mothers, aunts and cousins for life in the mother's home-range or an overlapping range. By contrast, the young stags leave the hind group at two years old and wander for another two years before settling with other stags on their own ground usually apart from hinds. These stag groups have less cohesion than the hind groups and gradually dissolve in autumn at the onset of the rut, when one by one the stags move to their rutting areas, often over a distance of several miles, to the other side of the island. There the roaring contests take place, and Rum echoes with the sound of their deep, throaty voices. They often come to blows with antlers locked, occasionally inflicting severe injuries; an old stag might have fought forty to fifty rutting battles in his life and sustained many scars. However, continuous fighting for a harem, though very much in the character of the dominant stag, is not in his best interests. Firstly, he stands a good chance of injury, and secondly, he expends valuable energy which is vital to see him through the cold famine of winter. Stags that can maintain the highest rates of roaring tend to be dominant.

During the winter between November and March the plane of nutrition on Rum falls and the deer starve; though they still graze the withered vegetation they get little nourishment. In April the first flush of green comes to the sea-meadows by the shore, and there lean animals often graze in mixed herds. The early spring nourishment provided by the draw-moss on the wet heaths of moor-grass, deer hair grass and cotton grass is also attractive in April; the first green shoots of these grasses and sedges are palatable, but not so their stiff grown leaves. The rapid increase in food in April and May is accompanied by the casting of antlers and the onset of growth of the new antlers in 'velvet'.

As spring passes into summer the deer move to rush meadows and to higher ground; away from biting flies they peacefully graze the grassy out-washed fans and gulleys, upwards to the mountain tops. The basalt hills of Bloodstone and Fionchra and the limestones of Monadh Dubh have excellent greens frequented by deer in summer, and when the highest pastures on the island over the shearwater grounds on the summits of the cuillin take growth in early summer the deer also move there. In June, the hinds drop their calves, usually choosing habitat with deep cover of grasses, rushes and heather, and in August the stags cast the 'velvet' from their antlers, which then harden and become both the symbols and weapons of challenge. As summer passes to autumn there is a resurgence of growth in the sea-meadows, to which the deer return to complete their provisioning before the rut and the first storms of winter, and the last nutritious food of the year is found among the heather.

The detailed story of the red deer of Rum has been pieced together over 30 years by a succession of workers whose names are written in the extensive literature which the study has yielded. There is no doubt that the fundamental biology of red deer (and other related species) has been greatly advanced by this work, and our enhanced understanding of the processes which govern their life should enable us to manage red deer in a variety of ways—from the truly wild animal of the mountain to the domesticated deer of farm or park.

Sea Eagles

It is testimony to the wild, shy character of the golden eagle (*Aquila chrysaetos*) that it has survived the persecution of centuries in Britain, and now enjoys full protection. By comparison, the white-tailed eagle or sea eagle (*Haliaetus albicilla*) is by nature much more confiding to man, and was exterminated in Britain at the beginning of the 20th century. The last pair nested in Skye in 1916.

In the past the sea eagle lived in the Hebrides in ecological conditions very similar to the present day but with important exceptions. These include persecution by shepherds, gamekeepers and collectors, and though the illegal killing and taking of eagles and their eggs has been greatly reduced, persecution of today is in constant scrutiny by the RSPB, police, and the general public. Also, the ability of eagles to raise young is inversely related to concentrations of pollutants in their food. Coastal eagles feeding on seabirds and fish may accumulate damaging amounts of these toxic substances (eg DDT and PCBs), which did not exist in former times when the sea eagles bred in the Hebrides. In 1968, George Waterston and Johan Willgohs of Bergen, who believed a reintroduction of the sea eagle to Scotland would be a great triumph for wildlife conservation, made an unsuccessful attempt at reintroduction on Fair Isle. A much more sustained effort over several years was clearly required.

The decision by the Nature Conservancy Council in favour
of the reintroduction of the sea eagle to Scotland was therefore
a finely balanced one to which Lord Dulverton gave crucial
support. The project was started on Rum in 1975. For eleven
years an annual batch of eight-week old nestlings was collected
under licence in Nordland by the Norwegian naturalist Harald
Misund, and transported by the Royal Air Force from Bodo to
Kinloss, Moray. From thence the birds were taken to Rum for
rearing and release into the wild under licence by the project
officer John Love. From the beginning the project was a fine
example of teamwork between the Nature Conservancy
Council, Royal Society for the Protection of Birds, Royal Air
Force, World Wide Fund for Nature, Scottish Wildlife Trust,
Institute of Terrestrial Ecology, and the Norwegians. It is
described in *The Return of the Sea Eagle* (Love, 1983).

J. A. Love releasing a young sea-eagle for its first flight in the wild on Rum. Between 1975 and 1985, 82 young sea-eagles were released from this rock above Loch Dornabac (Photo J. M. Boyd)

The Bodo district in Norway is very reminiscent of the
seaboard of West Inverness. The view that we described of
Skye and the Small Isles from Mallaig closely resembles that of
the sea-eagle islands Landegode, Helligvaer and Bliksvaer

from Bodo. The ecology is also similar in detail, but there is a difference of about 10° of latitude, with different day-lengths and breeding conditions. The confiding nature of the sea eagle is evident, when they can be seen scavenging in Bodo harbour, and nesting in accessible sites close to human habitation. They also nest at high density, as on Karlsoyvaer where the birch woods are similar to those on the Garvellachs, Raasay and South Rona. Nests are found in crevices on high vertical cliffs and pine trees above the fjords in sites typical of golden eagles in Scotland. The species prospers in Nordland, and the few young taken for the Rum project (single birds were taken from eyries possessing two eaglets) pose no threat to the sea eagle in north Norway.

If the birds could be given living space in the Hebrides the portents of reintroduction were good. However, there were a number of other unanswered questions to be put beside that concerning the toxic effects of pollutants. Would people with guns, traps and poisons in Scotland kill these huge, often low-flying and rather fearless birds (wingspan up to 3m, weight up to 7.25kg)? Would ravens, crows, greater black-backed gulls and fulmars (which seriously oiled one of those released in Fair Isle) harrass and cause the death of the newly fledged eagles? Would the resident golden eagles prevent the young sea eagles establishing feeding and breeding territories? Would the techniques of rearing and release cause the young birds to be 'imprinted' on their handler and have difficulties in forming successful breeding pairs in the wild?

The first batch of four young almost brought the project to a halt. The single male died before release, and of the three females reared and released one was later found dead under an electricity cable in Morven. The remaining two survived. Fortunately the project was budgeted for five years based on the fact that the birds were unlikely to breed in the first six years of their lives. The doubts of the critics and the jibes of the cynics were not strong enough to stop it, and since then it has gone from strength to strength. The techniques of transportation, caging, feeding, handling, release, provisioning and observing the birds in the wild all improved with experience. The project was extended, and over the period 1975 to 1985, 85 young eagles from Norway were transferred to Rum. Three died in captivity and 82 (43 females and 39 males) were released at the same rock beside the road above Loch an Dornabac. Seven (3 males and 4 females) died soon after release and a few others may have died unnoticed. Sadly, two were poisoned, one of which was four years old and approaching breeding condition.

The young eagles remain in the vicinity of the release site for a few weeks, and a few have settled in the Small Isles. Others have wandered far: south to Ireland, north to Caithness and throughout the Hebrides. The first birds were ready to breed in 1980–81; in 1980 birds were seen carrying sticks; in 1981 a crude nest was built close to the site used by sea eagles a century before, and between 1982 and 1984 there were several breeding attempts each year which failed because of infertile or broken eggs. This was possibly to be expected in young birds breeding for the first time, however. Other breeding pairs may have gone unrecorded. In 1985 at least four pairs attempted to breed, and the first Scottish-bred sea eagle for almost 70 years flew in the Hebrides. In 1986, two more were fledged, in 1987, three and in 1988, two. In 1988, eleven pairs (about a quarter of the birds reintroduced) attempted to breed, and in 1989, three pairs reared five young. The total number of Scottish-bred birds fledged so far is 13. All the birds are young; with growing numbers in breeding condition and with growing experience of the birds in breeding, prospects of a successful reintroduction are good.

The return of the sea eagle to the avifauna of Britain is on its way. Unlike the osprey which returned naturally, the sea eagle has been physically brought back by a scientific and technical endeavour. In the minds of those of us who conceived and ran the project, there was never any doubt that the qualities of the Rum National Nature Reserve as the point of introduction were the best in the country and that we would require to keep the supply of recruits coming from Norway for at least five years. In the event the recruitment continued, thanks to Captain Misund, for ten years and was discontinued on the year of the fledging of the first Scottish sea eagle in the new population. The project proceeds with the care and protection of breeding pairs towards a viable population by the end of the century.

St Kilda—Island of World Heritage

One of the pleasures of visiting St Kilda is to walk contemplatively through the ruins and meadows of the old village (Fig. 43). Even to those who know little of its history, the sight of the place instils a sense of wonder, while to those who are well-read on St Kilda, the place is positively haunted, with, in every direction, the signs of a vanished race of people.

To the few surviving natives, the St Kilda of their childhood will never return. Even to those of us who knew the deserted islands in the early 1950s when the sad sight of the derelict village was eased by an all-pervading sense of wilderness, the place is not the same. Today the sights and sounds of the modern army garrison and the stream of summer visitors tend to dispel the sequestered quality of the St Kildan experience of those former days. However, many more are now able to enjoy St Kilda, and it is still a pleasure to take the Keartons' book *With Nature and a Camera* (1897) to St Kilda to relish Richard's

Fig. 17
Location map of St Kilda

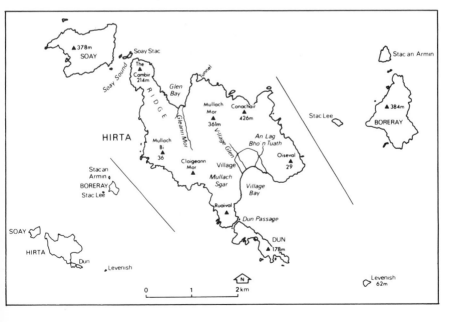

description and to stand in the exact spot of Cherry's photographs, placing again the St Kildans upon their island.

On small lonely isles, people and wildlife live in a microcosm; that's what makes them attractive to archaeologist, historian and scientist alike. St Kilda is at once superb in natural and cultural qualities succinctly stated in the *Nomination of St Kilda for inclusion in the World Heritage List* (Secretary of State for Scotland, 1985). Its 'world' status in wildlife heritage results from its vast seabird populations, its indigenous fauna of mice and wrens and its Soay sheep. However, the natural history of the islands is inextricably intertwined with the history of the St Kildans over many centuries; to appreciate the wildlife, one must also appreciate the people.

The St Kildans

Who were the first St Kildans? We can only make an informed guess. As the Stone-age and Bronze-age peoples moved northward into the Hebrides, from 6,600 to 2,400 years ago, so more and more islands became settled. It is logical therefore that in due time, a people accustomed to sea-going in small craft and blessed with an ameliorating climate, would reach St Kilda, but the spread of human settlement throughout the islands may have taken many centuries to accomplish. Cottam (1979) points to the absence of neolithic artifacts, indicating that the first St Kildans were probably Bronze Age people. However, he gives a word of caution on datings of artifacts at St Kilda since very little bronze actually reached these remote outliers. He suggests that, though St Kilda may have been visited by the hunter-fisher cultures (for seals and seabirds, including the great auk), it did not become settled until the arrival of pastoralists, who may have brought the ancestors of the Soay sheep. The earliest dating (radio-carbon) of human occupancy comes from boat-shaped settings of stones in An Lag Bho'n Tuath in Village Glen, *c.* 3,850 BP.

The Bronze-Age builders of the Callanish stone circle about 3,600 years ago enjoyed a warm, dry climate. Long periods of settled weather were probably much more dominant in island life than they are today, and the 80km passage from the Harris Sound or Loch Roag would be a much less daunting prospect than it has been in historical times. Further archaeological research may shed light on the first shadowy inhabitants, who probably long-predated the arrival of the Norsemen with their ocean-going vessels which made access to St Kilda much easier and safer, and carried larger cargoes of livestock, foodstuffs and people.

The history of St Kilda is written somewhat inscrutably upon the face of the islands in many generations of stone and turf structures and, less conspicuously, in soils, vegetation and fauna. The Village Glen and Gleann Mor are the main centres, but structures are present throughout Hirta even on the most unlikely cliff terraces and on all the other islands. Stac an Armin has many 'cleits' (drystone huts used for drying hay, turf and birds) and other structures, and Stac Lee has a small stone shelter tucked into its south-west wall. However, it is to the village that we must look for the testament of St Kildan culture. The modern intrusion of the army installations has been strictly limited from the beginning in 1957 to localities at the eastern end of the Village Area, the beachhead, the summits of Mullach Mor and Mullach Sgar and in the route of the road linking all those sites. It is one of the great achievements of the NTS, NCC and the army that, despite the disruption caused by military activity in such a small island, so little of its antiquities have been damaged or lost. The National Trust for Scotland has also reconstructed the church, schoolroom, factor's house, feather store and five cottages, and has consolidated the walls of other cottages, blackhouses and byres, 'cleits' and walls. The manse is now used as the Sergeant's Mess. In outward appearance none of the buildings have been changed from the pre-evacuation time prior to 1930.

Village Glen is a reliquary containing the artifacts of almost four millenia: boat-settings of stones, stone circles, cairns and

The 'Hardrock' operation of 1957 showing the tented camp in the Village meadows and a landing craft discharging on the beach. A construction squadron of the Royal Air Force built the Army base on Hirta, St Kilda in 1957–58 (Photo J. M. Boyd)

platforms dating from the Bronze Age to Christian times: the remains of an earth house or 'souterrain' possibly from the Iron Age about 1,700 years ago, denotes another cultural epoch which in turn was replaced by a new immigrant people who built round corbelled houses with separate living and sleeping compartments. The Calum Mor House in the Village, the Amazon's House in Gleann Mor and the Staller's House on Boreray together with many other corbelled remnants, may have belonged to this period.

The Norse influence came at that time, and though many of the place names are Norse and there have been Norse artifacts found on Hirta (notably two oval brooches indicating a woman's grave of the 10th century AD), the occupancy of St Kilda by Viking settlers was possibly light enough not to have displaced the native communities. Though the St Kildans may have from time to time been reduced or even expelled by disease and starvation over the centuries, the Norse names and the corbelled-building culture lived on into medieval times, when the main settlement was located at Tobar Childa under Glacan Conchair where a few medieval houses survive (one with a beehive sleeping chamber) among more recent 'cleits'. A causeway ran from the landing place (where the feather store was built in the 19th century) to Tobar Childa. This is the village that Martin saw when he visited Hirta in 1695.

In the 1830s the Rev Neil Mackenzie persuaded the St Kildans to build a new generation of houses in the pattern of the Hebridean *tigh dubh* or blackhouse along a new causeway some 200m nearer the sea. He also had a head-dyke built around the village and had the land between the Amhuinn Mor and the glebe sectioned into 19 runrig strips (Fig. 18). This signalled the end of the corbell-building, and thereafter all 'cleits' and drystone buildings were built with perpendicular walls exemplified by the large 'cleits' immediately behind the 'street.' However, the 1830s conformation of houses in the village street was short-lived, for in the 1860s the laird had 16 three-roomed, gavelled cottages built between the blackhouses, many of which thereafter became byres or stores. The present church and manse were built in the 1830s, the factor's house and the feather store in the 1860s and the schoolroom in 1898.

The evacuation of St Kilda is one of the social ironies of this century, and is best described by Tom Steel in *The Life and Death of St Kilda* (1975). The native community had possibly survived (with some enforced breaks in occupancy because of epidemic and starvation) for over 2,000 years and failed by 25 years to see its 'salvation' with the arrival of the Armed Services in 1956. In truth, the events at St Kilda in the past 30 years would have served to modernise the entire scene of *any* existing

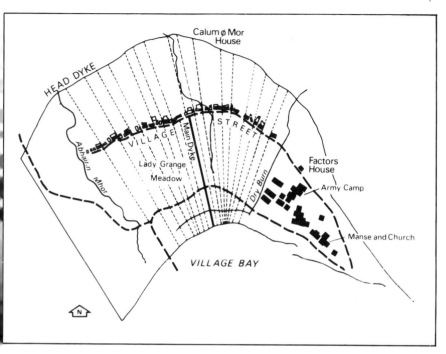

native community, and much of old St Kilda that now remains, could easily have been swept away.

As it is, the human scene has changed. For the few ancestral Gaelic-speaking families, there are now unnumbered short-term individual inhabitants. For the old culture, the remains of which are skilfully curated by the National Trust for Scotland, there is the 'high tech' of the army, upon which most other visitors to St Kilda ride pick-a-back. Nonetheless, when one is on one's own with the seabirds in the vastness of cliff, cave and stack, one is back in old St Kilda—in that timeless place where the frailty of human life is seen against the enduring rock of ages.

Fig. 18
Map of the Village of St Kilda in 1860 showing the unenclosed strips of land running from the shore to the head dyke with the cottage of each strip placed along the 'street' (St Kilda Handbook, National Trust for Scotland)

The Rock of Ages

St Kilda is a freakish little archipelago of four cliff-bound islands (Fig. 42)—Hirta (638ha., summit 420m), Soay (99ha., 378m), Boreray (77ha., 384m) and Dun (32ha., 175m)—about 70km west of the Outer Hebrides. There are also numerous stacks of which Stac an Armin (196m) and Stac Lee (172m) are by far the largest. Boreray and the two great stacks are a satellite group some 6km to the north-east of the main cluster of islands. The islands are the eroded fragments of a Tertiary volcano, thrust through the Precambrian and Mesozoic rocks at the edge of the Hebridean shelf some 60 million years ago. Fig. 19 shows a simplified geological map of the islands (Harding *et al.*, 1984). A mass of granite (the hills of Conachair and Oiseval in east Hirta with the remainder drowned in the Boreray Passage) is emplaced in a context of older gabbro (west coasts of Hirta and Dun, Glen Bay and all of Soay, Boreray and the great stacks). The gabbro and the granite are rocks of sharply contrasting character, and between them there is a zone of rocks of intermediate character known as the Mullach Sgar Complex—dolerites veined with microgranite (well seen in the Quarry), breccias, and inclusions of gabbro, possibly ruptured from the crust when the granitic magma was emplaced. The boundary between the granite and mixed rocks of the Complex can be clearly seen on the storm beach and in the buildings and head dyke of the village; the pale cream-coloured granite occupying the eastern end of the beach and hinterland while the remainder is made up of grey mixed rocks. The resulting volcanic massif has thereafter been faulted and intruded by dykes and sills or sheets, which are visibly shown on the seaward faces of Oiseval and Conachair.

Fig. 19
*Geological map of St Kilda (*St Kilda Handbook. *National Trust for Scotland)*

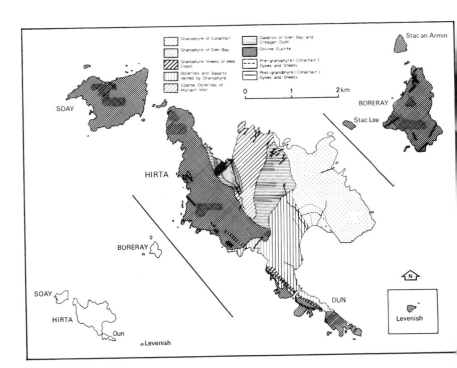

It is difficult to measure the extent of the St Kilda volcano, for unlike those in Skye, Rum and Mull, the lava fields which may have been extruded at the St Kilda centre have all been eroded away. The St Kilda islands are but small vestiges of a crustal mass which has been planed down by ice, water and weather to a depth of 1km or more. Between Hirta and Boreray there is a submarine platform at a depth of 60m, indicating a post-glacial erosion surface and possibly substantial changes in sea level and a drowned landscape. The cliffs descend sharply to this level, and are said to be pitted with submarine caves positioned at previous sea levels.

The topography is largely the result of the Quaternary glaciation and post-glacial marine erosion, but also reflects the rock structure. The granite weathers differently from the gabbro, and both are different from the dolerites of the dykes and sills. In broad silhouette, even as seen from distant North Uist, the granite hills of Conachair and Oiseval appear as smooth paps compared with the ragged outline of the surrounding ridges and islands of gabbro. Many of the dykes and sills are 'softer' than the rock into which they have been intruded, and this has resulted in large sea caves and tunnels (of which that at Gob na h'Airde is the grandest and the most accessible), chasms like the 'mauvais pas' at Gob Scapinish on Boreray, and natural arches like those around Gob an Dun. Faults provide lines of weakness exploited by the elements, resulting in such bold features as the chasm between Hirta and Dun, the Cambir isthmus and the gorge of the Amhuinn Mor, while others probably occur in the seabed in the Soay Sound, and between Boreray and the great stacks. The granite displays vast impending drapes of vertically jointed rock on the seaward faces of Oiseval and Conachair, overhanging the high-arched portals of caves as if constructed to 'plumb and square', and the great perpendicular wall of Conachair falls over 400m in this suite of cliffs. By comparison the gabbro is a capricious jumble of mighty bastions, pinnacle ridges and steep bevelled slopes, descending erratically to the sea.

The signs are that St Kilda may have stood proud of the Quaternary ice sheet but was probably ice-bound for most of the year and possessed a small valley glacier in Village Glen, which holds small moraines and together with Glen Mor, many periglacial features. There are fine exposures of glacial till on the 8m cliff behind the storm beach, and on the 20m bayside cliff of Ruaival and its stream gorge. The chronology of these drifts indicates a mild climatic interlude about 25,000 years ago (Middle Devensian) between two glaciations, the second of which was perhaps the more severe since it produced the glaciers and the devastating frost-shattering of the rocks,

giving rise to the extensive screes and blockfields of which
Carn Mor, Ard Uachdarachd, Tigh Dugan on Soay, Stac an
Armin, and the citadels of Ruaival and Point of Dun are prominent features. The mild spell is represented by a 20cm bed of
pollen-bearing sands derived, it is thought, by the fluvial
reworking of organic silt from the earlier glacial till.

It is testimony to the fine stature of A. M. Cockburn, who did
the first geological survey of St Kilda in 1927–28, that his work
(1935) has needed no major amendment and has formed the
solid basis for all that has been done since. Cockburn and his
friend John Mathieson, who drew the first OS map, saw the
community of St Kilda (1928) in its dying years and were indeed
fortunate to have the company of the St Kildans in their
reconnaissances to all the islands. The Oxford-Cambridge
Expedition of 1931 experienced the excitement of the uninhabited islands but did not have the St Kildans to assist them,
and were denied access to the even more wonderful solitudes
of Boreray and Soay.

Home of the West Wind

In its solitude upon the face of the ocean and standing tall with
its head in the clouds, St Kilda has a climate all its own. There
has been no long-term, consistent weather record of St Kilda;
the closest stations are at Benbecula and Butt of Lewis, 80 and
110km distant, which are the two windiest stations in the British
Isles. St Kilda lies close to the track of the Atlantic depressions
moving north-east from mid-ocean to the Norwegian Sea, and
winds, mainly from the south and west, are sometimes very
strong. Benbecula has recorded over a decade an average
annual wind speed of 24km/h. The St Kilda figure is probably
much higher because of the closer proximity to the coursing
storm centres and to the Venturi and severe drafting effects of
the islands rising starkly and abruptly in the rip of the wind. All
these factors combine to make St Kilda possibly the windiest
place in the British Isles.

There was a run of 33 months of parallel recordings between
Benbecula and St Kilda following the landings of 1957. Out of
900 days, St Kilda had 212 (21.4%) with winds of gale force.
(Force 8 on the Beaufort Scale: over 63km/h) compared with
124 (12.5%) for Benbecula. Gusts of 209km/h were recorded at
Mullach Sgar (213m above sea-level) in January 1962. Sea-
spray is blown over the islands in gales, and the chloride content of St Kildan soils varies from 30 to 321mg/100gm of soil
compared with 2mg/100gm of soil taken from a garden in
Edinburgh.

The first saucer-shaped antenna erected by the army on Mullach Mor was about 5m in diameter and was not encased in a dome. For overwintering it was turned edge-on to the prevailing wind and provided with an angle-iron frame firmly secured in concrete, but following a great storm the antenna together with its angle-iron frame was found bent almost horizontal! One of us was present in the first landing of the military 'operation Hardrock' in April 1957 and saw the task force caught by a storm with much of the equipment lying loose in the fields. There was devastation in the camp, with men viewing the holocaust from the safety of 'cleits'; furniture took flight over hundreds of metres and much of it ended in the sea.

The mean annual temperatures show a narrower range than at Benbecula; St Kilda is up to 2°C warmer in winter and cooler in summer respectively, ranging from 6°C to 12°C. The mean daily range of temperature at St Kilda is the narrowest in Britain (except for the Scilly Isles): 3°C in December and 6°C in May. The first frost occurs about 10th December (later than any other station in Britain) and the last about 20th March. Average annual rainfall is 1200mm, evenly distributed throughout the year with a much higher figure over the beclouded ridges. There is snowfall and lying snow for about 20 and 13 days respectively. Precipitation exceeds evaporation in all months except June, when both stand at about 80mm, and soils dry out for a few days. Humidity is consistently high throughout the year, averaging a little less than 90%, so it is little wonder that the St Kildan inventiveness applied itself to overcoming simultaneously the strength and wetness of the wind. The result, of course, is the thick-walled 'cleit', which withstands the strongest winds. Once used as a drying 'machine' for fodder and fuel it is today a dry lair for the Soay sheep.

The spring at St Kilda has spells of light to moderate northeast winds circulating a Scandinavian anti-cyclone, with the quietest and sunniest weather occuring in late May and early June, when the Hebrides are in a prolonged circulation of tropical maritime air. This is a moist flow however, with banks of sea fog. St Kilda makes its own cloud, and often when the wide ocean is sunlit, the islands have a cap or orographic cloud and are shrouded in drifts of snow-white mist. Such shrouds cut off sunshine and sometimes retard the recovery of the islands from their winter impoverishment, and plant growth is slow. Nonetheless, the lesser celandine (*Ranunculus ficaria*) is early to bloom in the lee cliff terraces and gullies, which are suntraps in summer, and where can also occasionally be found migratory painted ladies (*Cythia cardui*).

Seabirds of St Kilda

The most recent account of the seabirds of St Kilda (Tasker et al, 1988) updates *Birds of St Kilda* by Harris and Murray (1978) which cites 139 references to literature. In 1987, there were about 400,000 breeding pairs of 15 species of seabird (excluding eider) at St Kilda:

English	Scientific	Gaelic
Fulmar	*Fulmarus glacialis*	*Fulmair*
Manx shearwater	*Puffinus puffinus*	*Fachach*
Storm petrel	*Hydrobates pelagicus*	*Lauireag*
Leach's petrel	*Oceanodroma leucorhoa*	*Gobhlan-mara*
Gannet	*Sula bassana*	*Sulaire*
Shag	*Phalacrocorax aristotelis*	*Sgarbh-an-sgumain*
Great skua	*Stercorarius skua*	*Fasgadair-mor*
Lesser b-b gull	*Larus fuscus*	*Sgaireag*
Herring gull	*Larus argentatus*	*Glas-fhaoileag*
Great b-b gull	*Larus marinus*	*Farspag*
Kittiwake	*Rissa tridactyla*	*Ruideag*
Guillemot	*Uria aalge*	*Eun-dubh-an-sgadain*
Razorbill	*Alca torda*	*Coltraiche*
Black guillemot	*Cepphus grylle*	*Gearra-glas*
Puffin	*Fratercula arctica*	*Budhaig*

St Kilda holds about 20% of the population of the gannets in the North Atlantic, 20% of the *grabae* race of the puffin, the largest colony of Leach's petrel in the eastern Atlantic, and the largest colony of storm petrels in Britain. Probably over 1% of the European stock of kittiwakes, guillemots, and razorbills breeds at St Kilda. The honours accorded to St Kilda by the world conservation movement for its many high qualities in natural and human heritage, reflect the great value which people everywhere place upon its seabirds.

The measurement of numbers of seabirds breeding at St Kilda is a formidable task both physically and intellectually. To reach the breeding sites and to endure the vertigo, seas and weather of St Kilda demands guts, and against this background, the design of survey and the interpretation of the data demands brains. Before the evacuation, dating back to the days of the Rev. Neil Mackenzie 1829–43, the sizes of seabird colonies were related to the harvest of eggs and birds which were taken annually. Mackenzie stated that up to 5,000 young were taken, but Sands (1878) who spent 14 months at St Kilda, recorded 89,600 puffins killed in 1876. The latter figure bears no comparison with the former, and with such records there is no reliable way of plotting the history of the seabirds and seafowling. In broad terms, however, it seems certain that by 1900 the annual harvest of thousands of birds and eggs was in decline, and by 1930 was almost in abeyance.

Among the most intrepid St Kildan seafowling expeditions were the ascent of Stac Biorach (73m), the rock-fang in the Soay Sound, for guillemots, and the noctural visits to the great stacks to kill adult gannets in spring, driven on by winter starvation. The St Kildans had none of the boating and climbing aids of the present-day, only sail and oars, bare feet and horse-hair rope. Who today will row 6km to Biorach, climb it without boots and rope, and row the 6km home, as did the young men of old St Kilda with their harvest of guillemots?

James Fisher (1943, 1948, 1952) was the pioneer of seabird survey at St Kilda in the modern era. Though he was only able to scratch the surface of the task during his short visits, he showed that there was no alternative to setting eyes on as many of the breeding ledges as possible and to build up a round impression based on the best possible count. His work on the gannetry, done mostly from the heaving deck of a yacht, was a stimulus to others who came after and who combined much more detailed, on-site work with aerial photography (Boyd, 1961; Murray, 1981).

However difficult the gannets are to count, other species are even more difficult. Yet strenuous attempts have been made to assess the orders of magnitude and fluctuations of the populations of fulmars (Fisher, 1952; Anderson, 1957 and 1962; Harris and Murray, 1978), guillemots and kittywakes (Boyd, 1960; Harris and Murray, 1978; Tasker, *et al.*, 1988), puffins (Flegg, 1972; Harris and Murray, 1977 and 1978), and to study

Fig. 20
Map showing the distribution of puffins at St Kilda (from Harris and Murray, 1979)

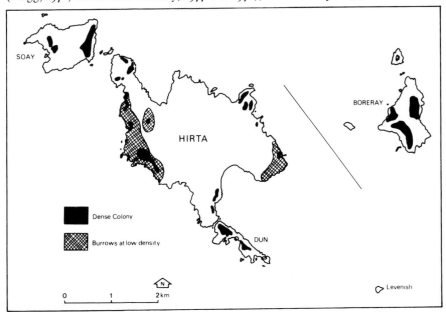

their feeding and reproductive biology. The challenge of this work carries with it the romance of a dramatic scientific quest on the edge of the world; few exercises in the survey of wildlife anywhere on earth can compare with the ascent of Stac Lee, the rock which Julian Huxley described (from the sea) as 'new to human experience'.

The significance of seabird research is not limited simply to the actual status of the species; it also sheds light on the ecology of the sea. The islands of St Kilda, which draw their throng of seabirds from the reach of the North Atlantic, are a focus of biological activity greatly disproportionate to their physical size. Changes in the chemistry of the sea and in standing stocks of marine organisms within the food-chain of seabirds are likely to be reflected in condition and numbers of the seabird species gathered at the breeding islands. There are already signs that seabirds carry high levels of pollutants such as poly-chlorinated byphenyls (PCBs), which become concentrated in seabird predators such as eagles of which none have bred at St Kilda since about 1835.

St Kilda has an especially sensitive ecosystem which could in future be used for the monitoring of the vast marine ecosystem. For example, industrial fishing of pelagic fish (herring, mackerel, sprat, pout and sand-eel) may cause measurable changes in the assemblies of gannets, auks and kittiwakes. Casting further afield, pollutants, including radio-active substances,

Species	Unit	Islands							Total
		Hirta	Dun	Soay	Bor'ay	StLee	StaA	Ot'r+	
Fulmar	aos	35,349	12,018	5,679	6,802	34	2,387	512	62,786
Manx sh'r	p/a	p	p	?	?	0	?	0	?
St. petrel	p/a	p	p	?	p	0	?	?	?
Ls. petrel	p/a	p	p	?	p	0	?	?	?
Gannet*	nests	0	0	0	24,676	13,521	11,853	0	50,050
Shag	nests	25	21	4	2	0	0	0	52
Gt. skua	aot	44	0	8	2	0	0	0	54
Lr. b-b. gl	aot	129	13	0	12	0	0	0	154
Herr'g gl	aot	14	4	0	38	0	0	3	59
Gt. b-b. gl	aot	13	12	5	15	0	1	10	56
Kittiwake	aos	1,719	1,231	1,306	2,923	245	326	79	7,829
Guillemot	ind	10,465	2,648	2,219	3,679	490	1,436	1,768	22,705
Razorbill	ind	1,221	1,809	263	252	15	237	17	3,814
Bl. guilt't	ind	0	10	2	5	0	0	0	17
Puffin	ob	10,800	41,600	115,000	63,000	0	100	1	230,501

+ = Levenish, Soay Stac, and Stac Biorach; aos = apparently occupied sites; p/a = presence/absence; aot = apparently occupied territories; ind = individual birds; ob = occupied burrows; * = 1985 data.

Table 10   Total numbers of birds on the islands and stacs at St Kilda from Tasker *et al* (1988).

entering the ocean and the food chain of seabirds might be brought to the green terraces of St Kilda and deposited there in the organic debris of the breeding populace. The terraces are grazed heavily by Soay and blackface (Boreray) sheep, which further concentrate the pollutants in the ewes' milk and ultimately in the bone-marrow of the lambs. A pollutant widely dispersed at low concentration could become highly concentrated within the island ecosystem, thus affording a sensitive means of detection of pollution. (The Chernobyl incident of 1986, and the increased levels of radio-activity that it caused in sheep stocks in Britain, points to the use of just such a biological monitor that the seabird islands have to offer.)

The distribution of breeding seabirds at St Kilda is shown in Table 10. The units in which the numbers of the various species appear to differ according to how the species presented itself to the counters in the field, and to aerial photographers.

Carn Mor is a large boulder-strewn terrace on the west of

Dr D. Boddington and Dr D. A. Ratcliffe at the 'cleits' on Stac an Armin in May 1959. The view is to the north wall of Boreray (Photo J. M. Boyd)

Mullach Bhi and the largest boulders are 7m broad. This is an underground labyrinth inhabited by burrow-nesting seabirds; by day the block-field with its steep, jutting landscape and ragged sheets of green *Holcus* is thronged with puffins and calling gulls, but at night the scene is transformed; the puffins are below ground and the gulls silent, but the night is full of the wings and calls of Manx shearwaters, storm petrels and Leach's petrels. Carn Mor is perhaps the most accessible site in Britain to witness all three species of nocturnal petrels. All three are also present on Dun where, on summer days, the visitor is given a fly-past by thousands of puffins swirling overhead in a great vortex and later settling in 'rafts' upon the sheltered waters of Village Bay.

The social structure of the seabird metropolis remains a mystery. What are the social factors that make the assemblies of the species so fragmented? Though there are manifestly suitable sites for breeding gannets in Hirta, Soay and Dun, what makes the gannets remain at Boreray and the great stacks (p. 15), and are the tenants of the many puffinries separate clans dispersing in winter to different sectors of the ocean? Guillemots (of which 10% are of the northern 'bridled' race) and kittiwakes have an affinity in nesting sites, which is well displayed on the west wall of Boreray and in the portals of sea caves on Dun.

Wrens and Mice

Awakening in the still calm dawn of a June day in the village, before the noise of the army generators smothered the gentle break of surf and call of birds, one might have been forgiven for thinking oneself at home in Midlothian. The torrential song of a wren on the factor's house chimney-head is a reminder of habitats of garden and wood far removed from St Kilda. It is a compelling call to action, and out early in the dew-drenched meadows, the sharp-eared ornithologist can walk the length of the village street and hear clearly ten cock wrens singing in their breeding territories, in company with piping oyster-catchers and drumming snipe. This is the St Kilda wren *Troglodytes troglodytes hirtensis*, which is larger with a longer bill, greyer and more heavily barred with paler underparts, than the russet-brown mainland race. Its song is also stronger, and has a somewhat different phrasing. Other distinct races occur in Shetland (*T. t. zetlandicus*), Fair Isle (*fridariensis*), the Outer Hebrides (*hebridensis*), and in other parts of Britain and Ireland.

There has been wonderment at the presence of the wren at

St Kilda since the earliest accounts. Those who had braved the sea-crossing were astonished that the tiny wren should have done the same and prospered. The differences between *hebridensis* and *hirtensis* are so great that the segregation of the two races possibly took place before the arrival of man in the Hebrides, and may have been assisted by land bridges with much shorter oversea-flying distances than exist today. There is evidence of vegetation on the land mass which is now St Kilda in middle Devensian times, about 25,000 years ago, and the wren may have been attracted there by the wooded habitat of that time.

How both the wren and the field-mouse arrived at St Kilda may always remain a mystery. Are these surviving relics of a bygone age of tree-covered islands, or have they been much later colonists? However, it is no mystery that having got there, these versatile animals have adapted beautifully to stark treeless St Kilda.

This adaptation has been discussed by Williamson (1958), who saw St Kilda as being far from austere for the wren, and the same might be said for the mouse. Though the weather is severe for those such as man and sheep whose business is on the land surface, it is not so for wrens and mice, whose business is largely underground. In good years there may be 230 pairs of wrens in St Kilda as a whole; they are present on Hirta (117), Boreray (*c.* 45), Soay (*c.* 45), Dun (*c.* 25) and Stac an Armin (*c.* 3). Only Hirta and Dun have been counted, and the highest

Fig. 21
Map showing the distribution of singing wrens on Hirta in 1957 (from Williamson and Boyd, 1960)

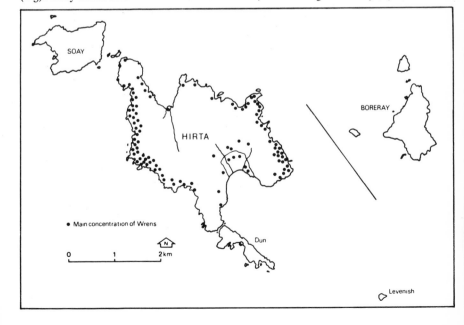

SOAY

HIRTA

BORERAY

• Main concentration of Wrens

N

0 1 2 km

Dun

Levenish

concentrations were associated with the puffin colonies, where there are large amounts of organic debris in a network of humid underground habitats slightly warmed by bacterial action, and lush green swards rich in invertebrates. In the village area the stoneworks and interiors of the cleitean replace the talus and burrow-system of the puffin slopes, and are probably much drier and warmer, especially when packed with bedded sheep. Many 'cleits' hold middens of sheep dung strewn with dead sheep which provide ample supplies of food for wrens and mice.

The abundance of food for the St Kilda wren in summer is much less than for the wren in the lowland broadleaved woodland, where the floor receives a rain of leaf-mining caterpillars. Thus the St Kilda wren breeds later and raises fewer second broods than those of wood and garden. The mainland cocks take little or no part in the feeding of young, while both members of the pair are required to feed the young at St Kilda, so the mainland cocks are therefore more polygamous than the St Kildan cocks. Nevertheless, the St Kilda wren's attempt to be polygamous and go through the ritual of building several 'cock nests', more than one of which is rarely occupied by a female. In years of warm, calm spring weather when the islands recover their green flush early, there may be more double-brooding, and this may result in an increase in the number of breeding pairs in the following year.

The wrens and field-mice of St Kilda possess the genetical features of distinct island races, as do the distinct species of the Galapagos. The description of the St Kilda wren by the ornithologist, Henry Seebohm (1884), as a distinct species *Troglodytes hirtensis*, was later revised as a sub-species. This placed a greatly enhanced value upon their skins and eggs which, together with those of the Leach's petrel, were keenly sought by the Victorian dealers and collectors. The St Kildans were not slow to realise what was happening and developed a trade, charging one guinea (£1.05) for an adult and 12s 6d (62.5p) for a juvenile (Williamson and Boyd, 1960), so much so that by 1894 it was thought—probably erroneously—that only 15 pairs survived. Concern mounted, and in 1904 an Act of Parliament was passed for the protection of the St Kilda wren and the Leach's Petrel.

The concern over both species was almost certainly ill-founded. Williamson and Boyd state:

. . . this craze for cabinet specimens could never have reduced its (the wren's) numbers significantly, for even after the collectors had got to St Kilda (no mean achievement in these days) the difficulties awaiting them in their task were well-nigh insuperable. For although a few pairs nested annually in the dry-stone cleitean where the St Kildans stored their peats and hay (and these wrens were always vulnerable), the bird's chief haunts are the inaccessible places along the towering, awe-inspiring range of the islands' cliffs. There they are, and always will be, secure from human depredation; and there, as it turns out, they are far from scarce.

No satisfactory measure of the size of the St Kilda wren population was achieved before Kenneth Williamson's dawn surveys of 1957.

The St Kilda field-mouse, like the wren, was first described as a distinct species *Apodemus hirtensis* by Barrett-Hamilton who a year later (1900) recast it as the sub-species *hirtensis* of the widespread species *A. sylvaticus*. Based on taxonomic differences, the St Kilda field-mouse is distinct from that of the remainder of the Hebrides, where the Rum field-mouse *A. s. hamiltonii* is also distinct both from St Kilda and the remainder of the Hebrides (Delany, 1964, 1970). Weights of *hirtensis* ranged from 29–40gms compared with 14–29gms for *sylvaticus*.

The St Kilda field-mouse may have been introduced by man, but the 'land-bridge' theory points to its having been there in advance of, and having survived, the last ice-age.

In 1955, when St Kilda was uninhabited, the field-mouse had no fear of man. Here, one walks across the chest of A. A. K. Whitehouse as he reclines among the ruins of St Kilda village in late May 1955 (Photo J. M. Boyd)

However, skeletal measurements indicate a closer identity with Norwegian field mice than with others, which points to a Norse origin rather than a relic left isolated by collapsing land-bridges (Berry, 1969). The fact that it is present on Dun and not on Boreray or Soay (Campbell, 1974) indicates that it may have been in the area before the collapse of the land-bridge joining Hirta and Dun, though it is just conceivable that it might have swum the Dun Passage and scaled the precipice! No similar doubt exists about the arrival of the St Kilda house-mouse which was also accorded the sub-specific status *Mus musculus muralis*; it arrived almost certainly in man's cargo.

Where they occur together in the presence of man, the house-mouse is a much more commensal animal than the field-mouse; at St Kilda the two occupied separate habitats as long as man was present to maintain the ecological difference. The house-mouse possessed the guile required to adapt to a comfortable life indoors; the field-mouse possessed the wilder instincts of a forager in the much more austere world of St Kilda's meadows and cliffs. When man left in 1930, therefore, a crisis may have ensued between the two populations. Deprived of the warmth and nourishment of the houses and out-houses, the smaller house-mouse had to venture into the open. Berry and Tricker (1969) have shown that *Mus* can survive in the presence of *Apodemus*, but the breeding of the former is disrupted causing a decline in numbers, and it is believed that such a decline in the population of *M. m. muralis* occurred following the evacuation in 1930. The Oxford-Cambridge Expedition of 1931 estimated the population at 25 mice, but none have been seen since, and it is now regarded as extinct. Today with much improved facilities for conservation and ecological knowledge, we could have saved *M. m. muralis*. A mouseless island might have been found with a sympathetic habitat, similar to Lunga in the Treshnish Isles (see p. 21) from which the inhabitants left in 1834 and which has a population of house-mice living in a field-mouse habitat, and no field-mice (Darling, 1940; Berry, 1983).

The future of the St Kilda field-mouse would be seriously jeopardised if rats were introduced to Hirta accidentally from army landing craft beaching at Village Bay. The only positive record of the black or ship rat (*Rattus rattus*) in the Hebrides is from the Shiant Islands where they seem to co-exist with the brown rat (*R. norvegicus*), but where there are no mice. The great swing from summer plenty in the puffinries to winter austerity would place mouse and rat in direct competition. Facing starvation winter after winter would soon reduce the numbers of mice, either by deprivation of habitat and food, or by actual predation by rats. Possibly the population of mice on

Dun might survive for a time, but rats are capable swimmers and are likely to cross the Dun Passage in due time. The status of the ground-nesting seabirds would also change in the presence of a large rat population. The introduction of rats therefore could seriously affect the 'heritage' properties which give St Kilda such a high rating in world conservation. No effort should be spared therefore in preventing the introduction of rats and, if an introduction is confirmed, steps should be taken to protect the field-mouse, possibly by its introduction to Soay or Boreray, where rats are unlikely to go and where it will do little or no harm to the habitat and sea birds.

Feral Sheep—Soays and Blackfaces

St Kilda possesses two breeds of sheep; the Soay, which takes its name from one of the islands, and the Blackfaces on Boreray. The Soays have been on St Kilda since pre-historic times, kept apart from improved breeds in the cliff-bound isle of Soay, while the Blackfaces are the survivors of the improved breeds kept apart on Boreray since the evacuation. When the St Kildans departed in 1930, they took with them their cross-bred blackface Cheviot sheep from Hirta leaving behind the Soays on Soay and the blackfaces on Boreray. In 1932, cross-bred stragglers on Hirta were shot, before a balanced flock of 107 Soays (42 rams and 65 ewes) were transferred from Soay to Hirta by a team of St Kildans returned for the summer. This was a great achievement since the Soays cannot be herded and must be run to ground individually on very steep slopes and man-handled down the cliffs to small boats. It is on this flock

Fig. 22
The fluctuations in the numbers of Soay sheep on Hirta 1960 to 1988, showing the proportions of rams, ewes, and lambs in the population in most years (from Prof. P. A. Jewell)

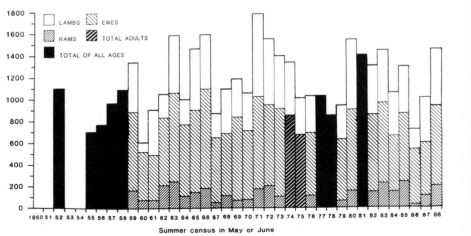

Summer census in May or June

that the present Hirta stock is founded, which since then have not been managed and have assumed the behaviour and population structure of wild sheep (Fig. 22).

The Soay sheep (*Ovis aries*) is the most primitive domesticated sheep in Europe, resembling those brought to Britain from continental Europe about 7,000 years ago by neolithic farmers. A description of these sheep and a comprehensive account of their biology is to be found in *Island Survivors — The Ecology of the Soay Sheep of St Kilda* ed. Jewell, Milner and Boyd (1974). Suffice it to say that there is no firm archaeological evidence of the date of arrival of the Soays at St Kilda. Sheep may have been introduced by the early colonisers of the Bronze or Iron Ages over 1,500 years ago, but there is also a strong possibility that sheep were taken to St Kilda by the Norsemen about 900 AD. The Soays may be the survivors of confluent primitive sheep cultures in the Hebrides; the Norse influence, seen in primitive breeds in Orkney, Shetland, Faeroe and Greenland,

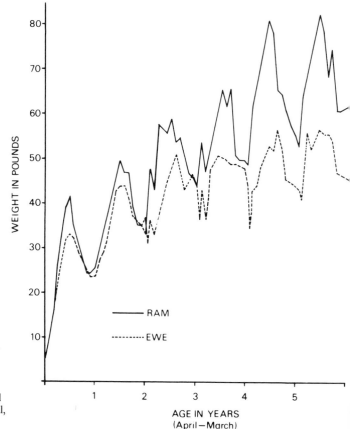

Fig. 23
Mean weights to ewes (dotted line) and rams (solid line) in relation to season and age in 1964 and 1965 (from Doney et al, in Island Survivors, *Jewell et al, 1974)*

may have come to an already-established sheep culture brought from Britain and Ireland in earlier times—the bones of the neolithic sheep from southern Britain resemble those of the Soay.

The Soays are small dark sheep which, when fully grown, are about 50cm in length (female) compared with 57cm in the blackface, with the Soay rams reaching 53cm. In autumn, 4-year-old Soay ewes and rams weigh on average 23 and 33kg respectively and 14 and 21kg respectively in early spring. Fig 48 shows the growth rate of ewes and rams, and the seasonal fluctuation in weights relative to seasonal nutrition in the pastures. These fluctuations in body weight are dramatic, 39% for ewes and 36% for rams.

There are two distinct phases of coat colour. About three-quarters of the Soays are dark brown and the remainder a light *café-au-lait* colour. In the Village area in 1964, there were 446 sheep of which 348 (78%) were dark. The 'type' specimen has a light buff-coloured belly, posterior, chin, trailing-edges of the legs and all of the lower legs (less distinct in the light phase). In 1966 (Grubb, 1974), of 1,835 on Hirta, 105 (5.7%) were self-coloured (completely uniform) of which 82 were dark, 23 were light and 85 (4.6%) had anomalous white markings. There were blazes on the forehead, spots on the nose and poll and below the knees, the horns of a few had longitudinal white stripes, and there were a few white-headed and piebald specimens. Most of these features have been observed in the original flock on the Isle of Soay. The inheritance of the coat colours and horns is complex and has been investigated by Doney *et al* (1974).

Full-grown rams have horns swept backwards and downwards in a single whorl, 49cm of outward edge and slightly out-turned at the tips. These show distinct annual growth increments, which reflect the seasonal cycle of nutrition. The first four years of horn growth are very obvious but thereafter are less distinct as the ram reaches its full size. About one in ten rams have scurs or small malformed horns. Ewes can be horned or polled; of 323 ewes 148, or 46%, were horned. The horns of ewes are 15cm and also show annual growth bands but much less clearly than do the horns of rams. About a quarter of the polled ewes have small scurs. Of 146 ewe lambs born in 1965 and 1966, 47 horned and 21 polled were born to horned ewes; 24 horned and 54 polled were born to polled ewes. The frequency of the horned/polled character of the ewe is reflected in the frequency of horned or polled off-spring produced, but the chance of the lamb inheriting its dam's horned or polled character is only about 2:1 in favour.

The Boreray sheep have a lineage on the island which goes

Boreray rams on the southern slopes of the island in late May 1979 (Photo J. M. Boyd)

back many centuries. Starting with the Soay-type they have probably been changed by introductions of new stock from Hirta, unlike those on Soay which, by historical quirk, have remained unchanged. Apart from a few largely unsuccessful sheep-catching forays, the Boreray sheep have been left almost untouched since before the St Kildans left in 1930. A few have been taken off for scientific study and breeding, but no new stock has been introduced. They are representative of the domesticated sheep of the Hebrides in the late 19th and early 20th centuries. M. L. Ryder in a personal note states that there is clear evidence that the Scottish Blackface reached St Kilda in the 1870s and replaced the 'Old Scottish Shortwool' or Dunface which were kept on Hirta for centuries, and predominated in Europe from 500 BC to 1500 AD, the character of which still survives today in Shetland and North Ronaldsay (Boyd, 1981a). Though called 'Blackface' the 'Boreray' breed is more correctly 'Tanface' and has been listed as an antique breed by the Rare-Breeds Survival Trust (Boyd 1981b).

Records show than on Boreray some 400 sheep live on about 55ha., of pasture—a stocking rate of 8 sheep per ha. compared with 1.7 sheep per ha. on Hirta (Soays) and commonly on the mainland, 1.5 sheep per ha. for hill sheep (Boyd, 1981; Bullock, 1983). In autumn when the population on Boreray is in good condition with rams weighing 45kg, ewes and yearlings 25 and lambs 12, the autumn biomass may be as high as 157kg per ha. and in late winter as low as 83kg per ha. The biomass of herbivores on the East African plains in a rainfall of 800mm/annum ranges from 48 to 199kg per ha. and is the highest in the world:

the Boreray ecosystem can be considered, therefore, as having a remarkably high turnover of biological productivity and energy.

The St Kilda sheep provide good opportunities for research. The flocks on Soay and Boreray are too remote to facilitate detailed work, but the population of Soays on Hirta is sufficiently accessible for continuous observation. They are also part of a comparatively simple ecosystem compared with populations of large herbivores elsewhere, living as they do within a small fine ecosystem in which there is no immigration or emigration; they have no competitors for the grazings nor predators of the adult stock (ravens, crows and large gulls may kill small lambs); no crop of lambs is taken, and the sex-ratio is naturally determined; there is no 'strike' of the blow-fly *Lucilia* spp. and the sheep are neither dipped nor shorn; neither are they directly interfered with by man or dog. Parasites are those of a closed system and are untreated. The Soays may have a feral genotype but they are in all other respects wild sheep.

The fluctuations in numbers have been followed since 1952, and continuously by a standard method since 1959 (Fig. 22). The annual cycle follows a strict pattern, with most adult mortality occurring in March followed by the birth of lambs, mostly in April. The population fluctuates in a roughly three to four year long cycle from 600 to 1,800 and survival is density-dependent.

The energy budget of the flock is all-important in seeing it through the rigours of winter and early spring. The degree of stress in winter is partly determined by the nutritional status of the flocks in the previous summer. When times of high density occur in a cold, wet and comparatively sunless summer, the pastures are not only depleted of green growth, but also the swards finish in autumn with a poor reserve in the rhizomes for growth in the following spring. This results in poor feeding for the sheep; adults die in February and March, and there is high mortality of lambs in April due to failure of lactation in the ewes. The energy budget in years of high density with poor weather is in serious deficit. Young rams are particularly prone to starvation, since much energy is lost in autumn in nuptial chases and copulation at the expense of a few weeks feeding. In 1978–80 in Village Glen, 72 ram lambs were castrated and 68 were left intact; in 1984, 42 castrates and 2 rams still survived; and in 1988 there were 38 and 2 respectively, clearly indicating the toll taken of the male population by the reproductive process.

In the grip of severe malnutrition, parasitism plays an important role in pushing the sheep to the point of death. The Soays are heavily infested with keds (*Melophagus ovinus*) and lice

(*Damalinia ovis*). Sheep ticks and blowflies have not been reported. The lambs and yearlings are heavily infested with the lungworm (*Dictyocaulus filaria*) and the older sheep with *Muellerius capillaris*, neither of which have so far been recorded from the Boreray sheep. The cysts of the tapeworm (*Taenia hydatigena*), the adult form of which occurs in dogs, is found without any obvious explanation of its life cycle on Hirta and Boreray, where there have been no resident dogs since 1930. There are heavy infestations of the nematodes *Trichostrongyle* spp., *Nematodirus* spp., *Bunostomum trigonocephalum*, *Trichuris ovis* and *Chabertia ovina*.

The three flocks of sheep at St Kilda seem to be in ecological equilibrium with their environment. The numbers are regulated by malnutrition, usually at times of high density, but at a level which does not cause obvious physical and biological damage to the habitat. They have been put there by man but have adjusted to become wild animals capable of surviving the stresses of inbreeding, physiological weakness, parasitism and malnutrition. The balance is delicate and interference, no matter how well-intentioned, might set the sheep against their habitat, setting in train changes in the soil, vegetation and in the sheep themselves. There will be those who say that the sheep are an artifact and should be removed, possibly to improve the lot of the burrow-nesting seabirds. However, to do so would substantially reduce the heritage value of St Kilda, removing assets of great cultural, historical and scientific interest. Removal of sheep would also reduce the diversity of plant life which their grazing sustains on the islands. There would also be those who would say that it is cruel to keep sheep at St Kilda in conditions of seasonal malnutrition. However, the sheep are now adjusted over centuries to meet the rigours of their world and shun any assistance which man might provide to carry them over the winter; by so surviving, they may create greater stress of numbers and environmental damage in succeeding years (Boyd and Jewell, 1974).

Bibliography

Ainslie, J. A. & Atkinson, R. (1937). On the breeding habits of Leach's fork-tailed petrel. *Brit. Birds.* 30, 234–248.

Anderson, A. (1957). Census of fulmars on Hirta, St Kilda in July 1956. *Scot Nat.* 69, 113–116.

Anderson, A. (1962). A count of fulmars on Hirta, St Kilda in July 1961. *Scot Nat.* 70, 120–125.

Anderton, R. & Bowes, D. R. (1983). Precambrian and Palaeozoic rocks of the Inner Hebrides. *Proc. Roy. Soc. Edinb.* 83B, 32–45.

Atkinson, R. (1940). Notes on the botany of North Rona and Sula Sgeir. *Trans. Proc. Bot. Soc. Edinb.* 30, 52–60.

Atkinson, R. (1949). *Island Going*, Collins, London.

Atkinson, R. (1980). *Shillay and the Seals*. Collins Harvill, London.

Ball, M. E. (1987). Botany, woodland and forestry. In *Rhum*, ed. T. H. Clutton-Brock & M. E. Ball. Edinburgh University Press.

Baxter, E. V. & Rintoul, E. J. (1953). *The Birds of Scotland*. Oliver & Boyd, Edinburgh.

Benn, S., Murray, S. & Tasker, M. L. (1989). *The Birds of North Rona and Sula Sgeir*, Nature Conservancy Council, Peterborough.

Berry, R. J. (1969). History in the evolution of *Apodemus sylvaticus* at one edge of its range. *J. Zool., Lond* 159, 311–328.

Berry, R. J. (1979). The Outer Hebrides: where genes and geography meet. *Proc. Roy. Soc. Edinb.* 77B, 21–43.

Berry, R. J. (1983). Evolution of animals and plants in the Inner Hebrides. *Proc. Roy. Soc. Edinb.* 83B, 433–447.

Berry, R. J. & Tricker, B. J. K. (1969). Competition and extinction: field mice of Foula, Fair Isle and St Kilda. *J. Zool., Lond.* 158, 247–265.

Bertram, D. S. ed. (1930). The natural history of Canna and Sanday, Inner Hebrides. *Proc. Roy. Phys. Soc. Edinb.* 32, 1–71.

Bignal, E., Monaghan, P., Benn, S., Bignal, S., Still, E. & Thompson, P. M. (1987). Breeding success and fledgling survival in the Chough. *Bird Study* 34, 39–42.

Birks, J. H. B. (1970). Inwashed pollen spectra of Loch Fada, Isle of Skye. *New Phytol.* 69, 807–820.

Birks, J. H. B. (1973). *Past and present vegetation of the Isle of Skye—a paleoecological study*. Cambridge University Press.

Birks, J. H. B. & Adam, P. (1978). Notes on the flora of Islay. *Trans. Bot. Soc. Edinb.* 43, 37–39.

Birks, J. H. B. & Marsden, B. J. (1970). Flandrian vegetational history of Little Loch Roag, Isle of Lewis. Scotland. *J. Ecol.* 67, 825–842.

Birks, J. H. B. & Williams, W. (1983). Late quaternary vegetational history of the Inner Hebrides. *Proc. Roy. Soc. Edinb.* 83B, 293–318.

Bland, K. P., Christie, I. C. & Wormell, P. (1987). The lepidoptera of the Isle of Coll, Inner Hebrides. *Glasg. Nat.* 21, 309–330.

Boddington, D. (1960). Unusual mortality of young puffins on St Kilda, 1959. *Scottish Birds* 1, 218–220.

Bonner, W. N. (1976). Stocks of grey seals and common seals in Great Britain. *Nat. Env. Res. Council Publ.* C16.

Booth, C. G. (1981). *Birds in Islay*. Argyll Reproductions Ltd.

Bourne, W. R. P. (1957). The birds of the Isle of Rhum. *Scot. Nat.* 69, 21–31.

Bourne, W. R. P. & Harris, M. P. (1979). Birds of the Hebrides: seabirds. *Proc. Roy. Soc. Edinb.* 77B, 445–475.

Boyd, A. (1986). *Seann Taighean Tirisdeach*. Cairdean nan Tiaghean Tugha.

Boyd, H. & Ogilvie, M. A. (1972). Icelandic greylag geese wintering in Britain in 1960–71. *Wildfowl* 23, 64–82.

Boyd, I. L. (1981). Population changes in the distribution of a herd of feral goats (*Capra* sp.) on Rhum, Inner Hebrides. *J. Zool., London.* 193, 287–304.

Boyd, I. L. (1984). The relationship between body condition and the timing of implantation in pregnant grey seals (*Halichoerus grypus*). *J. Zool., Lond.* 203, 113–123.

Boyd, I. L. (1985). Pregnancy and ovulation rates in two stocks of grey seals on the British coast. *J. Zool., London.* 205, 265–272.

Boyd, J. M. (1957). The ecological distribution of the Lumbricidae in the Hebrides. *Proc. Roy. Soc. Lond.* 66B, 311–338.

Boyd, J. M. (1958). The birds of Tiree and Coll. *Brit. Birds* 51, 41–56, 103–118.

Boyd, J. M. (1960a). The distribution and numbers of kittiwakes and guillemots at St Kilda. *Brit. Birds.* 53, 252–264.

Boyd, J. M. (1960b). Studies of the differences between fauna of grazed and ungrazed grassland in Tiree, Argyll. *Proc. Zool. Soc. London.* 135, 33–54.

Boyd, J. M. (1961). The gannetry of St Kilda. *J. Anim. Ecol.* 30, 117–136.

Boyd, J. M. (1962). The seasonal occurrence and movements of seals in North-West Britain. *Proc. Zool. Soc. Lond.* 138, 385–404.

Boyd, J. M. (1963). The grey seal (*Halichoerus grypus* Fab.) in the Outer Hebrides in October 1961. *Proc. Zool. Soc. Lond.* 141, 635–662.

Boyd, J. M. (ed.) (1979). The Natural Environment of the Outer Hebrides. *Proc. Roy. Soc. Edinb.* 77B, 561pp.

Boyd, J. M. (1981a). The Boreray sheep of St Kilda, Outer Hebrides, Scotland: the natural history of a feral population. *Biol. Conservation* 20, 215–227.

Boyd, J. M. (1981b). The Boreray blackface sheep. *The Ark* 8, 357–359.

Boyd, J. M. (1983a). Natural Environment of the Inner Hebrides: an introduction. *Proc. Roy. Soc. Edinb.* 83B, 3–22.

Boyd, J. M. (1983b). Two hundred years of biological sciences in Scotland. Nature Conservation. *Proc. Roy. Soc. Edinb.* 84B, 295–336.

Boyd, J. M. & Bowes, D. R. (eds.) (1983). The Natural Environment of the Inner Hebrides. *Proc. Roy. Soc. Edinb.* 83B, 648pp.

Boyd, J. M. & Campbell, R. N. (1971).

The grey seal (*Halichoerus grypus*) at North Rona 1959–1968. *J. Zool.* 164, 469–512.

Boyd, J. M. & Jewell, P. A. (1974). The Soay sheep and their environment: a synthesis. In *Island Survivors*, eds. P. A. Jewell, C. Milner & J. M. Boyd, pp. 360–373. Athlone Press, London.

Boyd, J. M., Tewnion, A. & Wallace, D. I. M. (1956). The birds of St Kilda, mid-summer 1956. *Scot. Nat.* 69, 94–112.

Bramwell, A. G. & Cowie, G. M. (1983). Forests of the Inner Hebrides—status and habitat. *Proc. Roy. Soc. Edinb.* 83B, 577–597.

Bullock, D. J. (1983). Borerays, the other rare breed on St Kilda. *The Ark* 10, 274–278.

Cadbury, C. J. (1980). The status and habitats of the corncrake in Britain 1978–79. *Bird Study* 27, 203–218.

Cadbury, C. J. (1988). Corncrake and corn bunting status and habitats on Tiree and Coll, Inner Hebrides. In *Birds of Coll and Tiree* (ed. D. A. Stroud). Nature Conservancy Council, Peterborough.

Campbell, R. N. (1974). St Kilda and its sheep. In *Island Survivors*, ed. P. A. Jewell, C. Milner & J. M. Boyd, pp. 6–35. Athlone Press, London.

Clapham, A. R., Tutin, T. G. & Warburg, E. F. (1975). *Excursion flora of the British Isles.* Cambridge University Press.

Clarke, J. G. D. (1946). Seal hunting in the Stone Age of north-west Europe; a study of economic prehistory. *Proc. Prehist. Soc. Lond.* 2, 12–48.

Clutton-Brock, T. H., Guinness, F. E. & Albon, S. D. (1982). Red deer: behaviour and ecology of two sexes. Chicago and Edinburgh University Presses.

Clutton-Brock, T. H., Guinness, F. E. & Albon, S. D. (1988). Red deer in the Highlands. Blackwell, Oxford.

Clutton-Brock, T. H. & Ball, M. E. (ed.) (1987). Rhum: the natural history of an island. Edinburgh University Press.

Cockburn, A. M. (1935). Geology of St Kilda. *Trans. Roy. Soc. Edinb.* 58 (21), 511–548.

Cottam, M. B. (1979). Archaeology of St Kilda. *St Kilda Handbook.* National Trust for Scotland.

Craig, G. Y. (1983). ed. *Geology of Scotland.* Scottish Academic Press.

Cramp, S., Bourne, W. R. P. & Saunders, D. (1974). *The seabirds of Britain and Ireland*. Collins, London.

Cunningham, W. A. J. (1983). *Birds of the Outer Hebrides*. Methuen, Perth.

Currie, A. & Murray, C. (1983). Flora and vegetation of the Inner Hebrides. *Proc. Roy. Soc. Edinb.* 83B, 293–318.

Darling, F. F. (1937). *A Herd of Red Deer*. Oxford University Press.

Darling, F. F. (1938). *Bird Flocks and the Breeding Cycle*. Cambridge University Press.

Darling, F. F. (1939). *A Naturalist on Rona*. Clarendon Press, Oxford.

Darling, F. F. (1940). *Island Years*. Bell, London.

Darling, F. F. (1944). *Island Farm*. Bell, London.

Darling, F. F. (1945). *Crofting agriculture*. Oliver & Boyd.

Darling, F. F. (1947). *Natural history of the Highlands and Islands*. Collins, London.

Darling, F. F. (1955). *West Highland Survey: an essay in human ecology*. Oxford University Press.

Darling, F. F. & Boyd, J. M. (1964). *The Highlands and Islands*. Collins, London.

Darwin, C. R. (1859). *On the origin of species by means of natural selection*. John Murray, London.

Delany, M. J. (1964). Variation in the long-tailed field mouse (*Apodemus sylvaticus* L.) in north-west Scotland. A comparison of individual characters. *Proc. Roy. Soc.* B161, 191–199.

Delany, M. J. (1970). Variation in the ecology of island populations of the long-tailed field mouse (*Apodemus sylvaticus* L.). In *Variation in mammalian populations* eds. R. J. Berry & H. N. Southern, pp. 283–295. Academic Press, London.

Dickenson, G. & Randall, R. E. (1979). An interpretation of machair vegetation. *Proc. Roy. Soc. Edinb.* 77B, 267–278.

Dobson, R. H. (1985). Manx shearwaters breeding on the Isle of Muck. *Glas. Nat.* 20, 491.

Dobson, R. H. & Dobson, R. M. (1985). The natural history of the Muck Islands, N. Ebudes. I. Introduction and vegetation with a list of vascular plants. *Glasg. Nat.* 21, 13–38.

Dobson, R. H. & Dobson, R. M. (1986). The natural history of the Muck Islands, N. Ebudes. 3. Seabirds and wildfowl. *Glasg. Nat.* 21, 183–199.

Doney, J. M., Ryder, M. L., Gunn, R. G. & Grubb, P. (1974). Colour, conformation, affinities, fleece and patterns of inheritance in Soay sheep. In *Island Survivors* eds. P. A. Jewell, C. Milner & J. M. Boyd, pp. 88–125, Athlone Press, London.

Duncan, U. K. (1968–70). Botanical studies in Coll & Tiree. *Proc. Bot. Soc. Br. Isles* 7, 298–299, 636–637; *Trans. Bot. Soc. Edinb.* 40, 482–485, 653–655.

Dunnett, G. M. & Ollason, J. C. (1978). The estimation of survival rate in the fulmar (*Fulmaris glacialis*). *J. Anim. Ecol.* 47, 507–520.

Dunnett, G. M. & Ollason, J. C. (1982). The feeding dispersal of fulmars in the breeding season. *Ibis* 124, 359–361.

Dunnett, G. M., Ollason, J. C. & Anderson, A. (1979). A 28-year study of breeding fulmars (*Fulmaris glacialis*) in Orkney. *Ibis* 121, 293–300.

Dwelly, E. (1977). ninth ed. *The illustrated Gaelic–English Dictionary*. Gairm, Glasgow.

Easterbee, N., Stroud, D. A., Bignal, E. M. & Dick, T. D. (1987). The arrival of greenland barnacle geese at Loch Gruinart, Islay. *Scot. Birds* 14, 75–79.

Eggeling, W. J. (1965). Check list of the plants of Rhum after a reduction or exclusion of grazing. *Trans. Bot. Soc. Edinb.* 40, 60–69.

Elton, C. S. (1938). Note on the ecological and natural history of Pabbay. *J. Ecol.* 26, 275–297.

Elton, C. S. (1949). Population interspersion: an essay on animal community patterns. *J. Ecol.* 26, 275–297.

Emeleus, C. H. (1980). *1:20,000 Solid Geology Map of Rhum*. Nature Conservancy Council.

Emeleus, C. H. (1983). Tertiary igneous activity. In *Geology of Scotland* ed. G. Y. Craig. Scottish Academic Press.

Emeleus, C. H. (1987). The Rhum Volcano. In *Rhum* ed. T. H. Clutton-Brock & M. E. Ball. Edinburgh University Press.

Ferreira, R. E. C. (1967). Community descriptions in field survey of vegetation map of the Isle of Rhum. Unpubl. report to Nature Conservancy.

Fisher, J. (1948). St Kilda: a natural experiment. *New Nat. J.*, 91–109.

Fisher, J. (1952). *The fulmar.* Collins, London.

Fisher, J. & Vevers, H. G. (1943). The breeding distribution, history and population of the North Atlantic gannet (*Sula bassana*). *J. Anim. Ecol.* 12, 173–213.

Fisher, J. (1966). The fulmar population of Britain and Ireland, 1959. *Bird Study* 13, 5–76.

Flegg, J. J. M. (1972). The puffin on St Kilda, 1969–71. *Bird Study* 19, 7–12.

Forbes, A. R. (1905). Gaelic names of beasts (mammalia), birds, fishes, insects, reptiles etc. Oliver and Boyd, Edinburgh.

Forest, J. E., Waterston, A. R. & Watson, E. V. (1936). The natural history of Barra, Outer Hebrides. *Proc. Roy. Phys. Soc. Edinb.* 22, 41–96.

Fuller, R. J., Wilson, R. & Coxon, P. (1979). Birds of the Outer Hebrides: the waders. *Proc. Roy. Soc. Edinb.* 77B, 419–430.

Gimingham, C. H. (1964). Maritime and sub-maritime communities. In *The vegetation of Scotland* ed. J. H. Burnett, Oliver & Boyd, Edinburgh.

Gordon, S. (1926). *The Immortal Isles.* Williams and Norgate, London.

Graham, H. D. (1890). *The birds of Iona and Mull.* Douglas, Edinburgh.

Grubb, P. (1974). Population dynamics of the Soay sheep. In *Island Survivors* eds. P. A. Jewell, C. Milner & J. M. Boyd, pp. 242–272, Athlone Press, London.

Gwynne, D., Milner, C. & Hornung, M. (1974). The vegetation and soils of Hirta. In *Island Survivors* eds. P. A. Jewell, C. Milner & J. M. Boyd, pp. 36–87. Athlone Press, London.

Hambury, J. (1986). *Agriculture & Environment in the Outer Hebrides.* Nature Conservancy Council Edinburgh.

Harding, J., Merriman, R. J. & Nancarrow, P. H. A. (1984). *St. Kilda: an illustrated account of the geology.* H.M.S.O. London.

Harris, M. P. & Murray, S. (1977). Puffins on St Kilda, *Brit. Birds* 70, 5.

Harris, M. P. & Murray, S. (1978). *Birds of St Kilda.* Institute of Terrestrial Ecology, Cambridge.

Harvie-Brown, J. A. & Buckley, T. E. (1888). *A vertebrae fauna of the Outer Hebrides.* Douglas, Edinburgh.

Harvie-Brown, J. A. & Buckley, T. E. (1892). *A vertebrae fauna of Argyll and the Inner Hebrides.* Douglas, Edinburgh.

Harvie-Brown, J. A. & Macpherson, H. A. (1904). *A vertebrate fauna of the North-West Highlands and Skye.* Douglas, Edinburgh.

Harwood, J., Anderson, S. S. & Curry, M. G. (1976). Branded grey seals (*Halichoerus grypus*) at the Monach Isles, Outer Hebrides. *J. Zool., Lond.* 180, 506–508.

Heslop-Harrison, J. W. (1937 and 1939). In *Proc. Univ. Durham Phil. Soc.* The flora of Raasay and adjoining islands, etc. 9, 260–304; the flora of Rhum, Eigg, Canna, Sanday, Muck, Eilein nan Each, Hyskeir, Soay, Pabbay, 10, 87–123; *et. al.* (1941) the flora of Coll, Tiree & Gunna, 10, 274–308.

Hewer, H. R. (1974). *British Seals.* Collins, London.

Hewson, R. (1954). The mountain hare in the Scottish islands. *Scot. Nat.* 67, 52–60.

Hogan, F. E., Hogan, J. & Macerlean, J. C. (1900). *Irish and Scottish Gaelic names of herbs, plants, trees etc.* Gill and Son, Dublin.

Hopkins, P. G. & Coxon, P. (1979). Birds of the Outer Hebrides: waterfowl. *Proc. Roy. Soc. Edinb.* 77B, 431–444.

Jewell, P. A., Milner, C. & Boyd, J. M. eds. (1974). *Island Survivors: the ecology of the Soay sheep of St Kilda.* Athlone Press, London.

Kearton, R. & Kearton, C. (1897). *With Nature and a Camera.* Cassel, London.

Kerr, A. J. & Boyd, J. M. (1983). Nature conservation in the Inner Hebrides. *Proc. Roy. Soc. Edinb.* 83B, 627–648.

Kruuk, H. & Hewson, R. (1978). Spacing and foraging of otters (*Lutra lutra*) in a marine habitat. *J. Zool., Lond.* 185, 205–212.

Lockie, J. D. & Stephen, D. (1959). Eagle, lambs and land management in Lewis. *J. Anim. Ecol.* 28, 43–50.

Love, J. A. (1980). Deer traps on Rhum. *Deer* 5, 31–132.

Love, J. A. (1983a). *Return of the sea-eagle.* Cambridge University Press.

Love, J. A. (1984). *The birds of Rhum.* Nature Conservancy Council, Edinburgh.

Love, J. A. (1987). Rhum's human history. In *Rhum* ed. T. H. Clutton-Brock & M. E. Ball. Edinburgh University Press.

Macaulay, K. (1764). *The History of St Kilda.* London.

Macleod, A. M. (1948). Some aspects of the plant ecology of the Island of Barra. *Trans. Bot. Soc. Edinb.* 35, 67–81.

MacLeoid, R. & MacThomais, R. (1976). *Bith-Eolas.* Gairm, Glaschu.

Martin, M. (1703). A description of the Western Isles of Scotland. Bell, London.

Mather, A. S. & Ritchie, W. (1977). *The Beaches of the Highlands and Islands of Scotland.* Countryside Commission for Scotland.

Mathieson, J. (1928). St. Kilda. *Scot. Geogr. Mag.* 44, 65–90.

Maxwell, G. (1952). *Harpoon at a Venture.* Hart-Davis, London.

Maxwell, G. (1960). *Ring of Bright Water.* Longmans, London.

McVean, D. N. & Ratcliffe, D. A. (1962). *Plant Communities of the Scottish Highlands.* Nature Conservancy Monograph No. 1. HMSO, Edinburgh.

McVean, D. N. (1958). Flora and vegetation of the islands of St Kilda and North Rona. *J. Ecol.* 49, 39–54.

Miller, H. (1879). *The Cruise of the Betsey.* Nimmo, Edinburgh.

Mitchell, B., Staines, B. W. & Welch, D. (1977). *Ecology of red deer.* Institute of Terrestrial Ecology, Banchory.

Monaghan, P., Bignal, E., Bignal, S., Easterbee, N. & Mackay, A. G. (1989). The distribution and status of the chough in Scotland in 1986. *Scot. Birds* 15, 114–118.

Monro, D. (1884). Description of the Western Isles of Scotland (Circa 1549). Thomas D. Morrison, Glasgow.

Murray, S. (1981). A count of gannets on Boreray, St Kilda. *Scot. Birds* 11, 205–211.

National Trust for Scotland (1979). *St Kilda handbook* ed. A. Small. NTS, Edinburgh.

Nature Conservancy Council (1974). *Isle of Rhum National Nature Reserve Handbook.* NCC, Edinburgh.

Nelson, B. (1978). The Gannet. T. & A. D. Poyser, London.

Nethersole-Thompson, D. & Nethersole-Thompson, M. (1986). *Waders: their breeding haunts, and watchers.* T. & A. D. Poyser, London.

Newton, I. & Krebs, R. H. (1974). Breeding greylag geese (*Anser anser*) on the Outer Hebrides. *J. Anim. Ecol.* 43, 771–783.

Nicholson, E. M. (1988). *The New Environmental Age.* Cambridge University Press.

Nicolaisen, W. F. H. (1976). *Scottish Place Names: their study and significance.* Batsford, London.

Ogilvie, M. A. (1983a). Wildlife on Islay. *Proc. Roy. Soc. Edinb.* 83B, 473–489.

Ogilvie, M. A. (1983b). Numbers of Greenland barnacle geese in Great Britain and Ireland. *Wildfowl* 34, 77–88.

Ogilvie, M. A. & Atkinson-Willes, G. W. (1983). Wildfowl of the Inner Hebrides. *Proc. Roy. Soc. Edinb.* 83B, 491–504.

Ogilvie, M. A., Atkinson-Willes, G. W. & Salmon, D. (1986). *Wildfowl in Britain* (2nd edit.). Cambridge University Press.

Owen, M., Atkinson-Willes, G. W., Salmon, D. (1986). *Wildfowl in Britain.* Cambridge University Press.

Parrish, B. B. & Shearer, W. M. (1977). Effects of seals on fisheries. Int. Coun. Explor. Sea, CM 1977/M:14.

Paterson, I. W. (1987). The status and distribution of greylag geese (*Anser anser*) in the Uists, Scotland. *Bird Study* 34, 235–238.

Perring, F. H. & Randall, R. E. (1972). An annotated flora of the Monach Isles NNR, Outer Hebrides. *Trans. Bot. Soc. Edinb.* 41, 431–444.

Pickup, C. (1982). A survey of greylag geese (*Anser anser*) in the Uists. Unpubl. report to the Nature Conservancy Council.

Poore, M. E. D. & Robertson, V. C. (1949). The vegetation of St Kilda in 1948. *J. Ecol.* 37, 82–89.

Randall, R. E. (1976). Machair zonation of the Monach Isles NNR, Outer Hebrides. *Trans. Bot. Soc. Edinb.* 42, 441–462.

Ratcliffe, D. A. (ed.) *A Nature Conservation Review.* Cambridge University Press.

Red Deer Commission (1961–75). *Annual Reports.* RDC, Inverness.

Reed, T. M., Currie, A. & Love, J. A. (1983). Birds of the Inner Hebrides. *Proc. Roy. Soc. Edinb.* 83B, 449–472.

Ritchie, W. (1966). The post-glacial rise in sea level and coastal changes in the Uists. *Trans. Inst. Br. Geogr.* 39, 79–86.

Ritchie, W. (1976). The meaning and definiton of machair. *Trans. Proc. Bot. Soc. Edinb.* 42, 431–440.

Ritchie, W. (1979). Machair development and chronology in the Uists and adjacent islands. *Proc. Roy. Soc. Edinb.* 77B, 107–122.

Sands, J. (1978). *Out of this World or Life on St Kilda*. Maclachan & Stewart.

Seebohm, H. (1884). New species of British wren. *Zool.* 8, 333–335.

Sharrock, J. T. R. (1976). *The Atlas of Breeding Birds of Britain*. T. & A. D. Poyser, Berkhamstead.

Spray, C. J. (1981). An isolated population of *Cygnus olor* in Scotland. *Proc. 2nd Int. Swan Symp., Sapporo* 1980, 191–208.

Steel, T. (1975). *The Life and Death of St Kilda*. Fontana, London.

Steel, W. O. & Woodraffe, G. E. (1969). The entomology of the Isle of Rhum National Nature Reserve. *Trans. Soc. Brit. Entomol.* 18, 91–167.

Stewart, M. (1933). *Ronay*. Oxford University Press.

Stewart, M. (1937). *St Kilda Papers 1931*. Private publ.

Storrie, M. C. (1981). *Islay: Biography of an Island*. Oa Press, Isle of Islay.

Stowe, T. J. & Hudson, A. V. (1988). Corncrake studies in the Western Isles. *RSPB Conservation Review*. 1988, 38–42.

Stroud, D. A. (1984). Status of greenland white-fronted geese in Britain, 1982–83. *Bird Study* 31, 111–116.

Stroud, D. A. ed. (1989). The birds of Coll and Tiree: status, habitats and conservation. *Scottish Ornithologists Club/ Nature Conservancy Council*, Edinburgh.

Sulloway, F. J. (1984). Darwin and the Galapagos. *Biol. J. Linn. Soc.* 21, 29–60.

Summers, C. F. (1978). Trends in the size of British grey seal populations. *J. Appl. Ecol.* 15, 395–400.

Summers, C. F. & Harwood, J. (1979). The grey seal 'problem' in the Outer Hebrides. *Proc. Roy. Soc. Edinb.* 77B, 495–503.

Swann, R. L. (1984). Birds of Canna. *Canna—the story of a Hebridean island*, J. L. Campbell, pp. 265–277.

Tasker, M. L., Moore, P. R., Schofield, R. A. (1988). The birds of St Kilda, 1987. *Scot. Birds* 15, 21–29.

Tansley, A. G. (1949). *The British Islands and their Vegetation*. Cambridge University Press.

Thom, V. M. (1986). *Birds in Scotland*. T. & A. D. Poyser, Calton.

Thompson, D. S. (1983). *The Companion to Gaelic Scotland*. Blackwell, Oxford.

Thompson, D. B. A. & Thompson, P. S. (1980). Breeding manx shearwaters on Rhum: an updated population assessment in selected areas. *Hebridean Nat.* 4, 54–65.

Vaughan, R. W. (1983). Seals in the Inner Hebrides. *Proc. Roy. Soc. Edinb.* 83B, 219–228.

Vose, P. B., Powell, H. G. & Spence, J. B. (1957). The machair grazings of Tiree, Inner Hebrides. *Trans. Bot. Soc. Edinb.* 37, 89–110.

Wanless, S. (1986). *A survey of numbers and breeding distribution of the North Atlantic gannet, Sula Bassana, etc. since 1969/70*. Nature Conservancy Council, Peterborough.

Watling, R., Irvine, L. M. & Norton, T. A. (1970). The marine algae of St Kilda. *Trans. Proc. Bot. Soc. Edinb.* 41, 31–42.

Watson, W. J. (1926). *The History of the Celtic Place-names of Scotland*. Blackwood, Edinburgh.

Welch, R. C. (1979). Survey of the invertebrate fauna of sand dune and machair sites in the Outer Hebrides during 1976. *Proc. Roy. Soc. Edinb.* 77B, 395–404.

Welch, R. C. (1983). Coleoptera in the Inner Hebrides. *Proc. Roy. Soc. Edinb.* 83B, 505–529.

Williamson, K. (1958). Population and breeding environment of the St Kilda and Fair Isle wrens. *Brit. Birds* 51, 369–393.

Williamson, K. & Boyd, J. M. (1960). *St Kilda Summer*. Hutchinson, London.

Williamson, K. & Boyd, J. M. (1963). *Mosaic of Islands*. Oliver & Boyd, Edinburgh.

Wormell, P. (1977). Woodland insect population changes in the Isle of Rhum in relation to forest history and woodland restoration. *Scott. Forest.* 31, 13–36.

Wormell, P. (ed) (1982). The entomology of the Isle of Rhum National Nature Reserve. *Biol. J. Linn. Soc.* 18, 291–401.

Wormell, P. (1983). Lepidoptera in the Inner Hebrides. *Proc. Roy. Soc. Edinb.* 83B, 531–546.

Wormell, P. (1987). Invertebrates of Rhum. In *Rhum* ed. T. H. Clutton-Brock and M. E. Ball. Edinburgh University Press, Edinburgh.

Index